Drawing
Animals

COLLINS

Drawing Animals

A STEP-BY-STEP GUIDE TO DRAWING SUCCESS

Peter Partington

David Brown

Darren Bennett

HarperCollins*Publishers*

First published in this edition in 1999 by
HarperCollins*Publishers*
77–85 Fulham Palace Road
Hammersmith, London W6 8JB

The HarperCollins website address is:
www.**fire**and**water**.com

00 02 03 01 99
2   4   6   7   5   3   1

Most of the material in this book was previously published in
Learn to Draw Farm Animals, *Learn to Draw Horses*, *Learn to Draw Cats* and *Learn to Draw Dogs*.

© HarperCollins*Publishers* 1999

Produced by Kingfisher Design, London

Editor: Diana Vowles
Art Director: Pedro Prá-Lopez
Designer: Frances Prá-Lopez

Contributing artists:

Farm Animals
John Davis, Robert R. Greenhalf, Martin Hayward-Harris, Roger Hutchins

Horses
Louise Mizen

Cats
Laura Andrew, James Dallas, Ryozo Kohira, Kyri Kyriacou, Lee Lawrence,
Ali Marshall, Philip Patenall, Jane Robertson, Amanda Williams

Dogs
Roger Hutchins

A catalogue record for this book is available from the British Library

ISBN 0 00 413380 3

Printed by Midas Printing Ltd, Hong Kong

CONTENTS

Introduction

When you first start to draw, you will discover that the basic techniques recur no matter what your subject may be. While there are obviously huge differences between various species of animals and the settings in which you find them, the same principles of drawing will hold good as you try to render your subjects in as lifelike a manner as possible.

Farm animals
Our rural landscape would be a bleak place without farm animals. These formerly wild creatures were domesticated by early man, and since then they have provided us with many of the staples of life we take for granted, such as meat, milk and clothing.

The farmers who raised these animals were proud of their achievements and often wanted pictorial records of their stock. Landowners, too, wanted paintings of their new breeds, and out of these trends grew a rural art, from peaceful pastoral scenes of cows and sheep to scenes of Highland cattle in turbulent weather.

Even in today's industrialized countryside there is plenty for you to draw. If you do not have easy access to rural areas, check with your local council to see if there is a city farm near to you.

Horses
Because of their generally placid nature, horses make excellent subject matter. There are many occasions when they remain relatively still, and these provide the perfect opportunity for drawing: you can, for example, study them at leisure when they are grazing in a field or when they are being groomed. Since horses have only a flat coat of hair, it is also easy to see their muscular structure, and this makes them fascinating creatures to draw from whichever viewpoint you choose.

Of all domesticated animals, horses are perhaps the most magnificent. To stand in proximity to a workhorse and experience its immense, muscular presence, its great strength and power, and yet at the same time be struck by its gentleness, can be an unforgettable moment. This book explains how to translate the power and spirit of a horse into a two-dimensional image that will convey the sense of the animal and its movement to the viewer.

Cats

As cats have now overtaken dogs in the popularity stakes as domestic pets, you should find no shortage of models on which to learn your drawing skills. Adult cats spend a large proportion of their time asleep, so you will have plenty of time to study them in repose. Kittens, however, are legendarily lively and they will provide you with excellent practice in doing swift sketches which can be worked up into more detailed drawings later.

Cats offer quite a challenge in their variety. Drawing the average domestic shorthair is no training ground for rendering a convincing portrait of a Persian, with its different facial shape and its body virtually lost in fur – the very opposite of the elongated, graceful shape of a Siamese. It is for this reason that cats offer endless interest for the artist with a bent for drawing animals.

Dogs

When you are looking for your first canine subject, choose a dog with very short hair so that you can more easily see its shape. Avoid dogs such as the Afghan hound and Old English Sheepdog, for example, until you have gained some experience and knowledge of a dog's anatomy and form. To begin with, it would also be advisable to avoid those breeds with unusual proportions, such as the Dachshund.

Dogs are generally extremely friendly animals, but caution must be applied when approaching one whose temperament you are not familiar with. A well-trained dog is easy to control, making it an ideal subject for drawing. However, even an untrained dog will often remain in one position for an appreciable time when it is sitting or lying down in a comfortable place, allowing you plenty of scope for close study.

Tools and Equipment

For the beginner artist, the huge range of drawing materials available may seem both exciting and daunting. All can be used to capture the diversity that animal life presents to us, but each tool does create a slightly different effect and mood, so some may be better suited than others for conveying the impression of a particular animal. When choosing your materials, the trick is to try out different ones and see which produces the most effective results for the drawing you have in mind.

Pencils
The everyday pencil is one of the most versatile of all drawing instruments, capable of producing rough, quick sketches as well as finely worked detail. Pencils come in various degrees of hardness, and it is this that affects the quality of line. The H range, ending with the super-hard 9H, creates a light, precise line ideal for careful studies of eyes, fur and feather. The

soft B range, culminating in the luxurious 9B, can provide rich, rough, textural effects and striking tonal variations. Midway between the hardness of the H range and the softness of the B range is the well-known HB all-rounder.

Some people prefer specialized pencils, such as clutch and propelling pencils. These come in a lower range of softness, but do not need to be constantly sharpened in order to produce a continuous and consistent line.

Coloured pencils enable you to draw and introduce colour simultaneously, while watercolour pencils produce a line which can be softened with a wash of water.

Explore the range of pencils by using as many different types as possible to discover what effects they produce and which suits your intentions and feelings best.

The medium-soft 6B pencil used to depict this Rough Collie on fine cartridge paper needed constant sharpening to produce the fine hairs of the dog's coat.

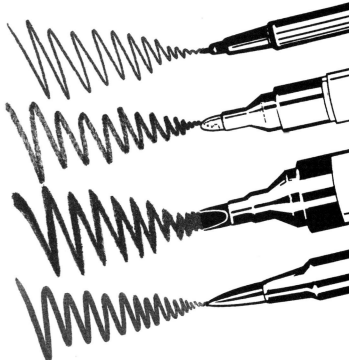

The softness of the down on these chicks was conveyed with the fine point of a ballpoint pen.

Overlapping strokes, a technique known as cross-hatching, were used to build up the tones.

Pens

Pens can produce a fluid, uncompromising line. They are available in several varieties, which produce slightly different effects and so are suited to different uses.

Fountain and dip-pens allow the artist to draw free-flowing or angular lines which vary in thickness depending on the pressure applied.

Ballpoint and technical pens produce a consistent, fine line. They are useful for sketching moving animals because they are quick to apply.

Felt-tip pens, in a range of widths, can create a similar effect, depending on their nibs.

Artist's Tip

Make sure you replace the tops on your felt-tip pens or the nibs may dry out. Wash out dip-pens after using or the ink will become encrusted on the nib.

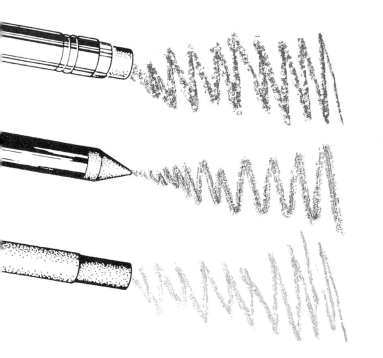

Pastels, crayons and chalks

The soft, textured quality of pastels and chalks offers an exciting alternative to the precision of pencils and pens. They work best on rough papers. The rich, powdery marks and lines which they produce can be smudged and blended. They are ideal for conveying the depth of thick fur or the sheen on a glossy coat because you can work light over dark, or allow the coloured paper base to show through.

Pastels and **chalks** can be used on their tips or on their sides to fill large areas quickly. Their rough, unfocused line can suggest light, movement and mood. They are particularly effective for lively, spontaneous drawing.

Oil pastels and **wax crayons** come in a dazzling array of colours, and allow you to introduce colour at the same time as line and contour. Soft oil pastels can be built up to resemble oil paint, but take care not to overwork wax crayon. Plan your picture carefully before you begin because these 'greasy' media are difficult to erase.

This tabby cat was drawn on coloured Ingres paper in pastel. The softness of this medium is ideal for giving an impression of fur rather than a detailed depiction.

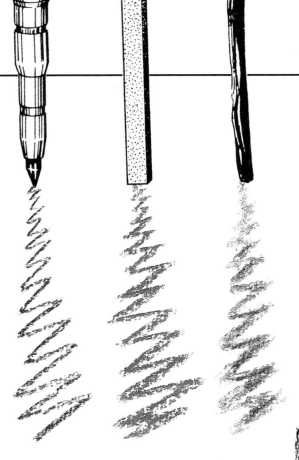

Conté crayon is similar in quality to pastel, but its slightly greasy texture makes it harder and less crumbly.

Charcoal traditionally comes in stick form. The softness of stick charcoal makes it perfect for working on a large scale, but it is rather messy, and drawings using this medium can easily become overworked. Charcoal is also made in compressed, pencil form for ease of handling. It produces a similar effect to the non-compressed variety but is more manageable if you wish to do smaller-scale work. To achieve a fine line with charcoal, gently rub the tip on sandpaper to produce a point.

Compressed graphite sticks look like large-scale pencil 'leads'. They come in various softnesses, and produce effects that resemble generous pencil strokes. They are a good tool to use if you want to work quickly, building up your drawing with a large number of lines.

To pick out highlights in a pastel or charcoal drawing, dab the surface with a putty eraser, or blend colours by rubbing them with your finger.

Charcoal is not a delicate medium but is ideal for making bold statements. Its strong, densely black quality perfectly captures the powerful form of this Rottweiler.

Artist's Tip

Charcoal smudges easily, so avoid resting your hands on your drawing while you are working. When you have finished, spray fixative on the drawing. This is available in cans or bottles, or may be blown on through a blowpipe.

Brushes and wet media

As well as adding colour or tone to a drawing, certain wet media, such as ink and watercolour, can also be used for drawing the lines that define form and outline. Depending on the type of brush they are applied with, they can produce a variety of line – delicate and flowing, short and broad, long and rhythmic.

The type of line you can create is determined by the shape of the brush tip, and tips come in a wide range of shapes and lengths. Among the most useful brushes for drawing are those that have long, pointed tips, the 'rigger' type being the longest. These produce long, fine lines. The length of the tips makes them very pliable, however, and they can be hard to control: brushes with short-tipped points are more manageable and can be used for fine detail.

3

5

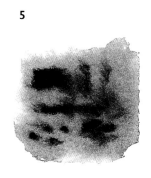

4

6

3 For an even layer of strong watercolour, lay darker washes over a light wash while still wet.

4 To prevent colours 'bleeding' together, let the first layer dry before adding the next.

5 For a soft, smudgy effect, paint watercolour on to paper that has been slightly dampened.

6 Ink or concentrated watercolour on damp paper will spread into swirls and blotches.

I

2

I These brush marks were made with *(from left to right)* a small, pointed brush; a flat brush; a large, pointed brush.

2 Watercolour tone can be progressively reduced by adding more water, as shown by these strokes using different dilutions.

Brushes with flat tips, either short or long, are the best type for covering large areas, or for producing extreme variations of line, in a similar way to a calligraphic pen.

The fibres or hairs used for brush tips vary in quality. Sable is the best-quality watercolour brush and gives very attractive results. Cheaper squirrel and synthetic fibres are quite adequate, however, and produce good-quality work. The tensile springiness of synthetic fibres can create fine, dynamic lines that are ideal for expressing the liveliness of certain animals. Brush-pens are good for this, too; they come supplied with a cartridge of coloured ink which ensures a consistent flow of colour.

Watercolour can be diluted with water in order to give transparent tones and gentle washes. When you want strong, vivid colours, reduce the amount of dilution.

Gouache is a form of watercolour that gives bold, opaque colour and dense coverage.

Acrylic paints can be diluted to create a watercolour effect; undiluted, they look like oils. They are good for strong, vibrant colour.

Ink may be applied with a pen to produce a line drawing or diluted and brushed on as a wash. The two methods may be combined in a line-and-wash drawing – but do the underlying drawing with waterproof ink or the wash may cause it to 'bleed'.

For wet media, you will need a palette for mixing and a couple of jam jars – one containing water for mixing your colours, the other for washing your brushes.

The watercolour outlines of this horse were applied with a fine pointed brush. The paper was then dampened in the patterned areas, and a wash was 'floated' on.

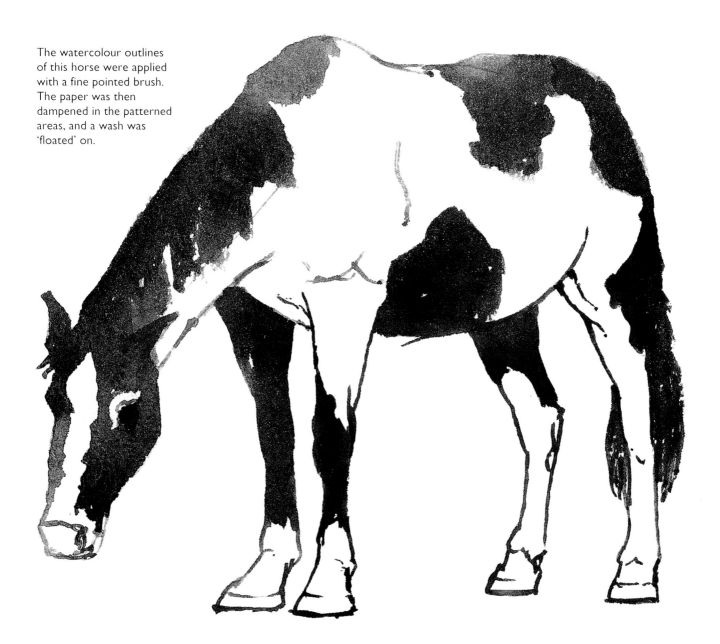

Newsprint is a very cheap paper, and therefore ideal for practising and for doing rough sketches.

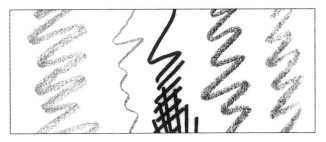

Tracing paper is semi-transparent, so you can lay it over other images and trace them.

Stationery paper, usually available in only one size, has a hard, smooth surface that suits a pen.

Cartridge paper is one of the most versatile of all surfaces. It usually has a slightly textured finish.

Surfaces to draw on

With experience, you will gradually learn which surface suits your style best, and which suits the medium you are working with. Try to experiment with different combinations of media and surfaces – it's exciting to explore the way in which each surface changes the appearance of each medium.

Watercolour paper is the most expensive paper you can buy. It may be made by hand or mould, and comes in different thicknesses that are measured according to the weight of a square metre. It is tough and absorbent, consisting partly or wholly of cotton and linen fibres which can give it an almost blotting-paper-like quality. It will withstand vigorous drawing and watercolour washes, and is acid-free so it will not go brown if left exposed to daylight.

Cartridge paper may be either cream or white, and is the most versatile, all-round surface for everyday drawing. You can buy cartridge paper in rolls or in sheets.

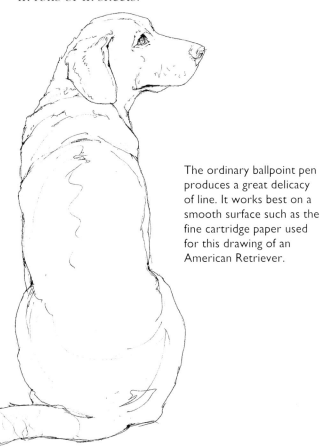

The ordinary ballpoint pen produces a great delicacy of line. It works best on a smooth surface such as the fine cartridge paper used for this drawing of an American Retriever.

Ingres paper, with a lightly ridged surface, suits pastel and charcoal, and comes in various colours.

Watercolour paper is ideal for wet media, being thick and absorbent with a rough surface.

Bristol board is firm and has a smooth finish that makes it a very suitable surface for pen work.

Layout paper is a semi-opaque, lightweight paper that is good for either pen or pencil drawings.

This tortoiseshell cat caught in a watchful pose was painted in watercolour on watercolour paper.

Cheap papers are another alternative. For example, the matt side of brown wrapping paper makes an interesting surface on which to work, as does photocopy paper and plain newsprint.

Blocks, **books** and **pads** are useful for outdoor sketching. Blocks are made of ready-cut and stretched watercolour paper on a card base. Books consist of watercolour or cartridge paper bound with a hard back. Pads are usually made of cartridge paper, spiral-bound or glued. They are available in two formats: *portrait*, or upright, and *landscape*, or horizontal.

Paper has three grades of surface: *hot-pressed* (smooth); *not* (not hot-pressed); and *rough* (textured). Smooth surfaces are best for pen and wash and detailed pencil work, while rougher surfaces suit bold work in pencil, charcoal or crayon. Pastels and chalks work best on special textured pastel paper because their particles cannot cling to smoother surfaces.

Watercolour papers often have attractive textures – 'laid' or 'wove' – according to the mould they are made in. This can add enormously to the interest of your work.

Farm Animals

Peter Partington

Choosing the Right Medium

1

The final result you produce depends not just on the medium you choose, but also the surface on which you have been working – a particular medium may look different on different surfaces. Experiment with various combinations to see what kinds of results you can create, and which combinations best suit your style and subject matter.

You may, for example, want to portray the details in an animal, in which case a drawing tool with a fine point such as a hard pencil, applied to a smooth surface, will fulfil your aim. Alternatively, you may want to express a sense of flow and movement, or give a more general impression of the animal as a whole. Here, the flowing line from a wet brush on watercolour paper will enable you to convey this feeling more easily. To create a sense of mood and atmosphere, the softness of charcoal is ideal.

Looking at examples

The pictures on these pages show a cockerel in the same pose, yet all look very different according to the medium and surface that has been used. Ballpoint pen on white card, as in the second drawing, for example, produces fine, crisp lines which are good for conveying the detail of fur, eyes, or feet. Compare this with the loose brushwork on wet watercolour paper or the charcoal on textured paper in drawings 4 and 5. The softness of these two combinations gives a sense of light, movement and mood.

From the examples on these two pages, you can see how, by exploring different combinations of medium and surface and then choosing the most appropriate, you can achieve the effect you want much more quickly.

2

1 Soft pencil on cartridge paper
2 Ballpoint pen on white card
3 Dip-pen and ink wash on thick cartridge paper

4 Brush-pen on wet watercolour paper
5 Charcoal on textured paper
6 Watercolour on watercolour paper

3

5

4

6

Farm Mammals

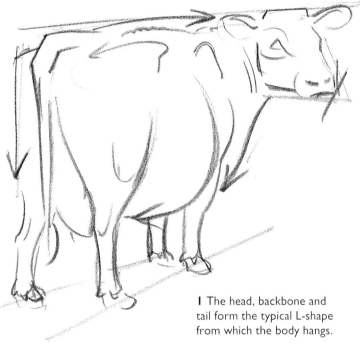

Cows, sheep, and pigs are the most familiar farm mammals and, of these, the milk-cow sums up all that is warm and secure in the farmyard.

Cows

The cow shown on this page is Kirsty, an Ayrshire – a breed which typifies the animal's angular 'wedge' shape that starts narrow at the front and widens out towards the rear, and provides a useful framework for your drawing. Here, the animal is seen from behind and the wedge is condensed. The full curve of the belly and rib-cage hangs down from the spine and the bony supporting limbs. The udder echoes this rhythm, and the tail provides a useful vertical.

1 The head, backbone and tail form the typical L-shape from which the body hangs.

2 I built up my initial sketch with charcoal to convey the body's roundness.

Head shapes

The shape of cows' heads varies, from the delicate and deer-like features of the Guernsey to the broad features of the great Charollais beef cattle from France. The little Guernsey has expressive brows, large black eyes, and a small nose; the Charollais, on the other hand, as you can see from the drawings below, looks altogether more robust.

When you draw this head, keep in mind its box-like form. Notice how the vertical sides of the cheeks almost form a corner as they meet the rather flat forehead and bridge of the nose. If you maintain this underlying structure as you develop your drawing, you will preserve the three-dimensional quality you need throughout the later stages of your cow 'portrait'.

1 I marked out the box-like structure lightly first, positioning the ears, eyes, and muzzle *(above)*.

2 I then worked into the drawing, suggesting the 'slab' sides of the cheek *(above right)*. I filled the eye with tone, leaving a white highlight.

3 Using a soft 8B pencil, I completed the drawing, indicating the curly top-knot and forehead as well as the crease-lines over the eye *(right)*. I then strengthened the whole head with more tonal marks, and left blank the shine on the nose.

Sheep

Gently grazing in green meadows, sheep form an essential part of the rural scene – and what typifies springtime more than new-born lambs?

There are many varieties of sheep, each having its own characteristics. The shape of each animal changes as the year progresses. The fleecy coat that develops towards winter makes a sheep's body appear more bulky, while still echoing the shapes of the limbs beneath. From beneath this bulk, the legs protrude like sticks. The thick collar of wool around the neck obscures its shape, so that head and body appear to merge. In early summer, however, the underlying structure of the animal's form is revealed when its woolly coat is shorn.

1 Doing a drawing of a lamb feeding from a ewe is a good way to compare their different shapes. Here, I began by sketching in the basic outlines in pencil.

Notice how the ewe's body forms a square, with only the lower part of her legs protruding beneath, and how the head sits at an angle on the body.

2 I then rounded off the corners in my basic sketch, and drew sweeping curves to indicate the way in which the coat follows the form of the body underneath.

3 When I was happy with my basic drawing, I used Indian ink and a no. 3 pointed brush to draw the first strokes following the guidelines, and to begin picking out the lamb's shape from that of its mother. I then worked into the drawing with diluted ink, and white gouache paint.

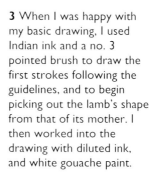

Notice the slant of the almond-shaped eyes and the set of the ears, low down on the head, in this soft charcoal study *(above)*.

Looking at the head

As well as the differences in size, body shape and markings, the shape of a sheep's head varies from breed to breed. Some, such as the Suffolk, have a fairly short, triangular face; others, such as the Dorset, have a high-bridged 'Roman' nose; some breeds have larger eyes than others.

From the front, a sheep's head forms a long triangle. In all sheep, the eyes lie much closer to the ears than imagined, and the eye socket forms an important feature, its bold shape emphasized by a bony eyebrow ridge. Be sure to stress this circular form, and to fit the eye shape within it. The eye also has a pronounced tear duct flowing towards the nostrils, which are linked to the lips in a Y-shape within the small muzzle. On either side of the nostrils the muzzle swells out.

A sheep's ears are leaf-shaped, and have a connecting bridge to the muscles on the top of the head which control them. From the side view, the mouth has a slight 'smile', and the small nostrils hardly feature.

A half-grown sheep: the ears are still proportionately large and the nasal ridge is becoming prominent *(left)*. The long, curved nose, high 'raised' brows, and pinched nostrils can give a sheep a haughty look. I used an 8B pencil for this drawing.

Artist's Tip

If you are having difficulty drawing the ears, make a fake ear to study. Fold a piece of paper in half and cut out a leaf shape with the fold down the middle. Try drawing it end on and from other angles to give you confidence when drawing the real thing.

23

Goats

These animals have angular shapes that make them wonderful subjects to draw. They are closely related to sheep but are leaner and more gaunt, feeding as they do on marginal land. Because goats are more assertive than sheep, it may be wiser to draw that billy-goat from outside its enclosure!

Most breeds of goat look similar, although some, such as the Nubians, have floppy ears. Their bone and muscle structure can be very apparent.

Use your pencil marks to emphasize the goat's angular shapes. Work into the drawing gradually with marks that suggest hair lying over the form and around the cylindrical neck.

1 I began by sketching in the structure of the body with simple angular lines *(above)*. Notice how the feet align to indicate depth.

2 Next, I introduced detail with pencil strokes that follow the body hair, gradually darkening them and using cross-hatching to suggest form *(above right)*.

3 In my finished drawing, large brows emphasize the characterful head *(right)*. The horns flow out of the crown of the head as a natural extension.

Pigs

A popular subject for the artist, these animals are very accessible for drawing when confined to their pens. They come in a wide variety of breeds from the hairy Tamworth to the attractive Gloucester Old Spot. Here, I have drawn one of the breeds of 'black' pig.

Their shape is simple – muscles and bones are concealed by ample flesh. Begin with a bean-shape, drawing from the wrist. The legs are shaped like old-fashioned pegs, narrowing down from the hams to the points of the trotters.

The pig's nose may be seen as an upturned heart-shape which fits over the lower jaw and is punctured by its two nostrils *(above)*. Pigs have small eyes.

  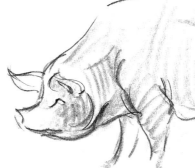

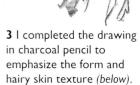

1 To begin my pig, I drew loose, curving lines around the bean-shaped body, and suggested the upper hams

and rib-cage. Notice the 'S' shape of the jointed limbs. I hung the head and the ears from the front of the body.

2 Working in further, I began to add curving lines to suggest the body's weight and roundness *(above)*.

3 I completed the drawing in charcoal pencil to emphasize the form and hairy skin texture *(below)*.

Artist's Tip

Keep your hand flexible and draw freely from the wrist in order to produce rhythmic, flowing lines. You don't have to keep your pencil point sharp – a slightly worn head will give you a variety of thicknesses of strokes.

Horses

There are still a few farms that employ working horses, and you can also see them at county shows and at Shire horse centres. Their form reflects their amazing strength and spirit.

To draw a farm horse, begin by sketching a square, placing the barrel of the body in the upper half. From this, pull out the massive curve of the neck and head. Use the vertical of the tail to work out the curve of buttocks and hind legs.

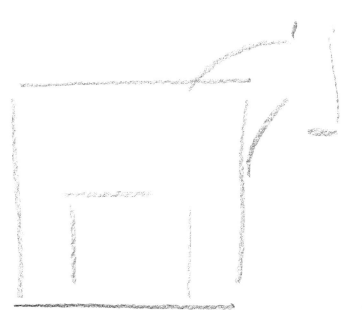

1 I first lightly sketched the square and the curve of the neck, marking off where I thought the head would be.

2 I then started drawing the rhythmic curve of the back and belly, indicating the width of the legs and suggesting how they link in with the body. The leaf-shaped ears and eye were added as markers.

3 Finally, to emphasize the contours of the body, I worked in tone with hatching strokes, leaving lighter areas for the gloss on the coat.

Rabbits

Wild and tame rabbits can usually be found about the farmstead. The tame ones come in many colours, shapes and sizes, from the giant Hollands and lop-ears to the miniatures.

When running, rabbits' bodies stretch out, but when sitting they retract into compact shapes like that of the rabbit below.

In side-view, a rabbit's head is almost a triangle, tilted slightly. The pointed end forms the small nose. The eye is large, and over it curls the large brow which can sometimes be seen to link up with the muscles that control the ear. The ears are roughly the same length as the head. Two leaf shapes can form the basis for ears. Your pencil strokes should imitate the directions taken by the fur itself.

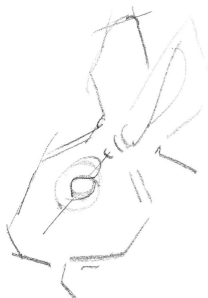

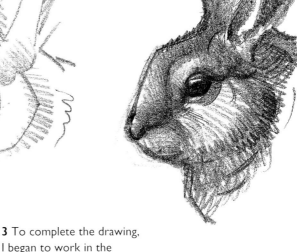

1 Two triangles, their points downwards, form the basic shapes of the rabbit's head and ears.

2 Working into the two triangles, I first drew the concentric circles around the eye, adding emphasis to the brow. I then worked into the eye, leaving a blank spot for the highlight.

3 To complete the drawing, I began to work in the tone, using my pencil strokes to follow and define the contours. Notice the lighter areas on cheek, nose and ear.

Artist's Tip

Use tone to convey an animal's three-dimensional form. Unworked areas left blank will appear to swell out, while darker areas will appear to curve away, and will add weight to the form.

In this drawing of a seated rabbit (right), notice how the body has become a series of concentric circles, and the head and ears a tear-drop shape.

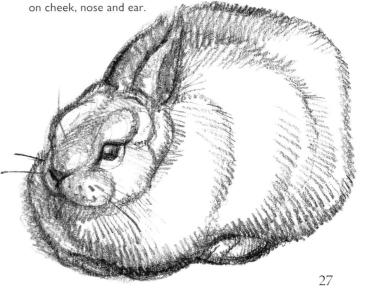

27

Farm Birds

Hens, ducks and geese are the most common feathered inhabitants of the farmyard, the hen being probably the most familiar farm bird.

Hens

As with other farm creatures, the simplest way of drawing a hen is to look for easy geometrical shapes which underlie the complex feathering.

The wing joint is folded quite forward under the hackles (neck feathers), and you can link this up with the saddle in a long 'S' shape. The saddle and tail often bulge over the tightly folded wings, and the flank feathers bulge nicely, too, giving the whole a very satisfying shape. The sturdy legs begin on a line with the base of the tail, and end in strong feet, suited to scratching.

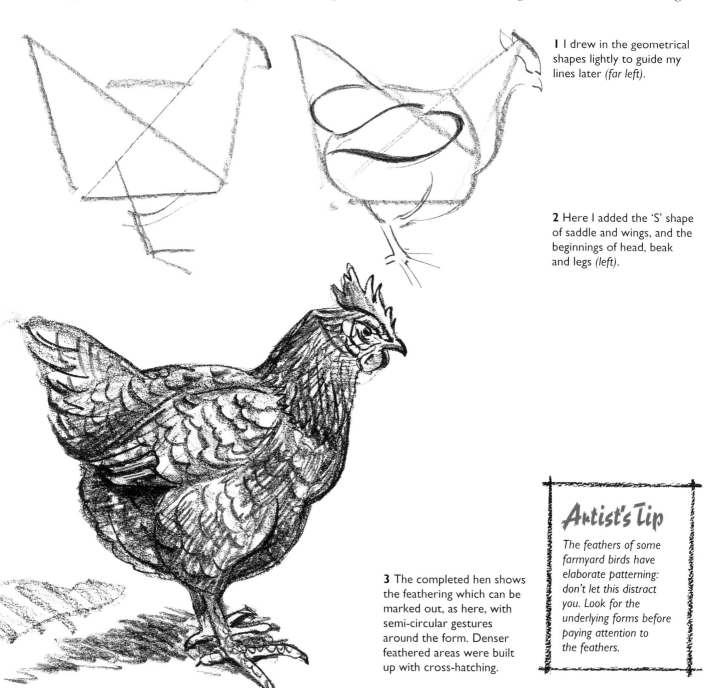

1 I drew in the geometrical shapes lightly to guide my lines later *(far left)*.

2 Here I added the 'S' shape of saddle and wings, and the beginnings of head, beak and legs *(left)*.

3 The completed hen shows the feathering which can be marked out, as here, with semi-circular gestures around the form. Denser feathered areas were built up with cross-hatching.

Artist's Tip

The feathers of some farmyard birds have elaborate patterning: don't let this distract you. Look for the underlying forms before paying attention to the feathers.

Doves were once
not just a decorative
addition to the farmyard,
but provided a source
of food. Simplicity is the
theme in this pencil and
watercolour wash drawing
of a resting dove.

Ducks

After the hen, the duck is probably the most familiar farmyard bird. There are various breeds of duck, in different shapes and sizes.

The breed I have chosen to show here is the Khaki Campbell. This flightless bird relies on its endearingly comic waddle to get itself around. Its tapering body begins with its elegant head and neck, gradually filling out towards its rounded rear, which is firmly placed on its short, strong legs and paddle-feet. In the pose shown here, you can see the striking 'S' rhythm running through its shape, which is given an extra fillip by the curly tail feathers.

1 Keeping my wrist loose, I drew sweeping lines to indicate the rhythms flowing over the head, down the body, and back up again.

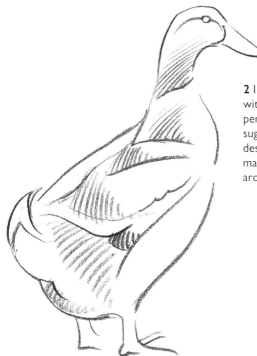

2 I added tone gradually with hatching strokes of my pencil. I used these lines to suggest contour and to describe how the feather masses wrap themselves around the body.

3 I completed my drawing by darkening certain areas to give weight and shape to the form – around the feet, under the tail feathers, and around the wings – varying the pressure on my pencil to create different thicknesses of line. I also strengthened the outline.

Geese

The domestic goose is similar in shape to the duck, and is descended from the wild Greylag. Some breeds are almost indistinguishable from their wild ancestor, while others are pure white or a mixture of the two.

Like that of the duck, the goose's body begins gracefully, but ends with a fat rear under the tail coverts. Its neck is long and can twist in a snake-like way. Its head is squarer than the duck's, and its bill more triangular, with a distinctive 'nail' on the end for cropping grass.

In profile, you can see how the goose's bill slots into the head between the rounded forms of cheeks and forehead. Notice how the pointed inner corner aligns with the eye *(right)*.

The goose has a long, elegant neck. From the base of the neck the body balloons out into a full, rounded form, slung low over the wide feet *(left)*.

The goose's neck feathers are pleated and fold into useful lines for describing movement. In some geese, the feathers are barred with the dun, scaly plumage of the wild bird, and these stripes provide an ideal opportunity for suggesting the roundness of the body. The big paddles of the feet give the bird a firm base.

Artist's Tip

Try to draw as much as you can from life. Even if your drawings are only sketchy, constant working from life will improve your grasp of the characteristics of each bird.

Structure and Form

Farm mammals are grass- and foliage-eaters. Grass takes a lot of effort to digest and it is the specialized digestive system of these mammals that gives them their characteristic bulk.

In the illustration below, you can see the massive rib-cage of the cow that contains the stomach and three other chambers, the largest of which is the 'rumen'. This contains bacteria which break down the woody content of the grass. The cow, like other 'ruminants', brings the grass up to chew it before finally digesting it.

Sturdy body
The cow's bones and muscles have to be very sturdy to support all this. The sinews join the muscles to the bones, and the muscles surround the tissues and bones to power the animal.

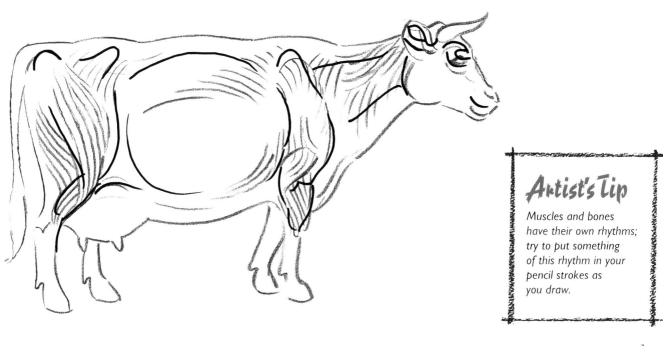

Artist's Tip

Muscles and bones have their own rhythms; try to put something of this rhythm in your pencil strokes as you draw.

The cow actually stands on its toes – the three-part bone structure enables the leg to fold easily and give good suspension. Observe the points at which the bones come close to the surface, and how this affects the surface shape *(above)*.

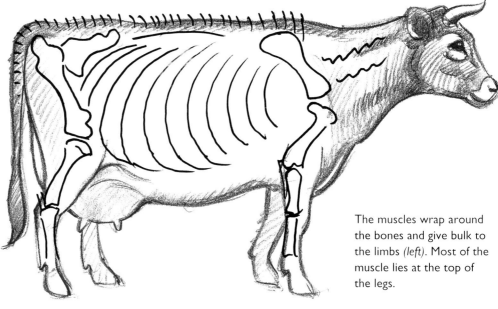

The muscles wrap around the bones and give bulk to the limbs *(left)*. Most of the muscle lies at the top of the legs.

Lambs are very active –
the legs reveal the springy
suspension system of
the three-part bone
arrangement in the limbs
(left). Their heads are big,
and their necks are strong.

Flexible legs

Compare the bulky body of the cow with that of the lamb above. Lambs are not as yet weaned on to grass, so their belly has not yet developed a bulky digestive system.

What is more clearly apparent in this young animal, though, is the zig-zag structure of the legs which enables these mammals to compress

and fold their limbs. The lamb can straighten its leg, or tense it ready to leap or run. The rear leg bends forward at the upper joint, like a human knee, giving dynamism to the animal's pose.

In resting posture, the front leg of the goat below is compressed and folded back, while the back leg stretches out forward. The other back leg will be folded under the body.

Goats have a bony
muscular structure which
reveals their anatomy.
For this reason, they make
good drawing subjects, such
as this floppy-eared Nubian
goat *(right)*.

33

Feather masses

Of all farmyard birds the hen is the most familiar, and this is the bird I have chosen to look at here. The domestic hen is descended from various species of Asian jungle-fowl which have been imported into the West throughout history. From these stocks, various breeds have been developed by man, in an infinite range of colours and shapes.

Whatever the bird's size and shape, however, the basic plumage and anatomy remain the same. Once you understand something of the feather masses illustrated here, the birds become much easier to draw.

The bulk of larger feathers lies around the tail, the saddle and shanks. The feathers get finer and more compact up to the head, which appears small in relation to the body. You can see how the feathers tend to overlap each other, like roof-tiles, from the head to the rear.

Wings and tails

Hens' wings are small and tucked in. The 'shoulders' are held forward under the neck. The impressive tail display – the 'sickles' – of the cockerel are not in fact tail-feathers but well-developed upper tail coverts. These grow out from above the tail and are supported in their upright position by the tail-feathers themselves.

The more dominant the cockerel, the redder and larger his comb will be. This begins right above the beak, while the wattles begin under it, sometimes joining the flesh around the eye.

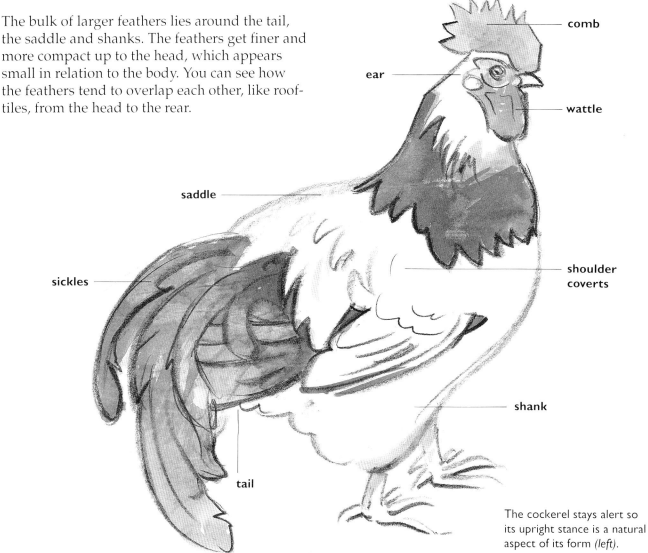

The cockerel stays alert so its upright stance is a natural aspect of its form *(left)*.

Underlying structure

The plumage of chickens conceals most of what is going on underneath. The leg muscles and bone emerge from the pelvis at the back of the knee, but this is totally concealed by feathers and lies close to the breast. The knee then joins the 'backwards' joint in an arrangement rather like that in the hind leg of a horse. The tarsus then appears from under the flank feathers, pointing forward to join the large scaly feet.

The bulk of the body lies over and ahead of the feet, which adds a forward momentum to the whole body. The wing bones are folded like an arm and tucked in under the neck. The neck itself is long and can be extended and contracted at will – the hackles (neck feathers) will expand and thicken the form as the neck folds back into the body of the bird.

The body of the hen is actually quite small under all its fluffy plumage (above). The bird plants its feet in a straight line when it walks. Most of the bulk lies ahead of the feet, creating a rocking waddle.

The feather masses on chickens are often clearly defined by colour and tone. This makes them useful subjects for studying plumage.

Hackles, wing feathers and upper tail coverts mask the underlying structure of the hen (left). Some breeds also have 'pantaloons' – bunches of feathers above the tarsus (ankle).

Proportion and Perspective

Your drawings of farm animals will have greater conviction if you get their proportions right. These vary, of course, from species to species, from breed to breed, and according to the age of the animal.

The effects of perspective
Although proportions remain constant in each animal, your viewpoint will change their appearance to the eye. For example, we all know that a cow further away will look smaller than one near at hand. This curious visual trick is called *perspective*, and can affect the proportions of an animal so that what you *see* differs from what you *know* – although you know that a cow has two pairs of legs of equal length, perspective may make the legs furthest away look shorter.

You can measure this visually, if necessary. The simplest method of doing so is to hold up a transparent ruler or lead pencil in front of your subject and mark the size of a part, say, the length of the head, with your thumb. You can then use this as your unit of measurement, and compare it with the size of other parts to check the animal's proportions. As your skills grow, your eye will begin to make these comparisons automatically, without mechanical help.

In the bull calf below, for example, you can see that its legs are still quite long in proportion to the body, and that its head is large. If you measure the length of its head, you will find that just over four 'heads' make up the length of the body. Similarly, its front leg goes into the length of its body about one and a half times.

I did this quick sketch of a bull calf rapidly with a soft-grade graphite stick.

Foreshortening

When you look at an animal from the front or rear, its parts 'telescope' together; this effect is known as *foreshortening*, and is illustrated in the drawing of young heifers below.

In this drawing, we are looking at these animals from in front and above – notice the distortions that occur. The bellies have almost disappeared, the rumps are higher than the heads, and the back leg of the heifer on the left starts level with the ears. Phenomena such as these are what you should be looking out for.

Seen from this viewpoint, the proportions of this cow *(above)* are extremely distorted, with a huge rear compared with a tiny head.

If you measured the heads of these heifers *(left)*, you would find that they are disproportionately larger than their bodies. However, our brains translate this distortion so that we 'read' their proportions as normal.

Different angles

The heads of farmyard animals – mammals, in particular – are formed of a fascinating series of curves, hollows, lumps and bumps. The rules of perspective come into play again here, affecting the shapes and proportions of eyes, ears, noses, and muzzles, depending on the angle from which you are viewing the animal.

When drawing an animal's head, it is very useful to use 'construction lines' – like the lines in the drawings below and opposite – to help establish the proportions of the various parts, and to site them correctly in the whole. As your skills improve, you will soon learn to visualize these lines without actually having to draw them.

Age differences

As with other parts of the body, the proportions of animals' heads vary depending on their age. In young animals, for example, eyes and ears tend to be larger in proportion to the rest of the head than in mature animals.

Your measurements will help to identify what age the animal is that you are looking at.

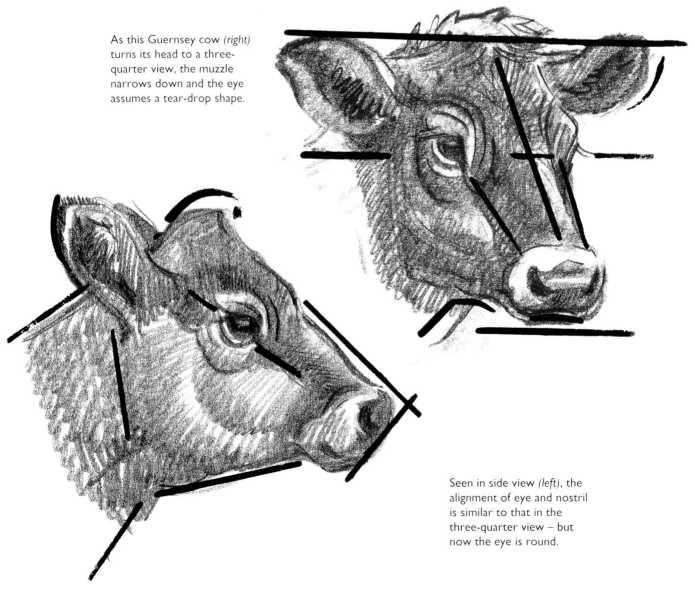

As this Guernsey cow *(right)* turns its head to a three-quarter view, the muzzle narrows down and the eye assumes a tear-drop shape.

Seen in side view *(left)*, the alignment of eye and nostril is similar to that in the three-quarter view – but now the eye is round.

1 This diagrammatic rendering of a calf's head shows it in terms of the most basic shapes, with lines to link the features *(above)*. Notice how, due to perspective, the ear on the far side is higher, and how the muzzle below the nostrils is foreshortened.

2 The finished drawing, still with some construction lines to show the alignment of key features *(above right)*.

Artist's Tip

You can sometimes buy quite good little models of farm animals, and these can be very useful to work from to improve your knowledge of proportion and perspective.

Viewed from a rear three-quarter view, this calf's muzzle is foreshortened *(right)*. The relative sizes of ears and eyes tell us that it is a young animal.

Proportions of birds

As with farm mammals, the proportions of farm birds vary depending on the bird's age and the observer's viewpoint. For example, the Khaki-Campbell duck on the right is full-grown, and its wings and body have reached full length. Its head and feet are smaller in proportion to its size than those of the ducklings below.

A side view of the characterful Muscovy duck is shown opposite. The relative proportions of head to body are shown in superimposed rectangles. The body itself suggests a cone shape with the sharp end at the tail, and, from side view, the facial features are not distorted.

As the same bird walks towards us, however, its cone-shaped body changes to become almost circular. We are looking along the face, which therefore shows the effect of foreshortening.

The structure of the body is very obvious in young birds *(below)*. It is the heads and feet which enlarge least as they grow.

As the same birds mature, the body grows larger, making the head and feet look proportionately smaller *(above)*.

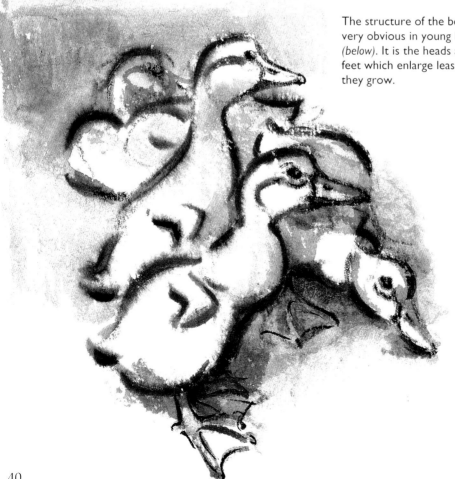

Artist's Tip

In side view, ducks' bodies have an underlying 'S' shape. The 'S' shape is more rounded in young birds.

1 & 2 From the front, the shape of the duck's body can be broken down into concentric circles *(right)*. The crop and breast conceal the wings and tail behind. As we look along the length of the duck's paddle-feet, they become narrower.

1 & 2 You can judge the relative proportions of head to body by casting imaginary rectangles around them. Note that most of the body is ahead of the legs. Proportions of eye to beak to head should be kept in mind to capture the character of this duck.

Looking at Features

Once you have learned about the broad outlines of farm animals, it is time to look more closely at their features – noses, ears, beaks, feet, and so on.

Farm mammals

The eating habits of farm mammals affect the shape of their features. The cow has a wide muzzle to accommodate the large tongue which crops the grass. The jaws of sheep are smaller,

as are the nostrils which fit neatly over the mouth-parts rather like a hare. As in many grazing animals, the eye is large and placed high on the head to keep a look-out for danger.

The pig eats anything available. Its upper lip curls slightly over its upper canine, and the nostrils are circular, with a sharper upper edge; the lower edge is moist and slightly shiny.

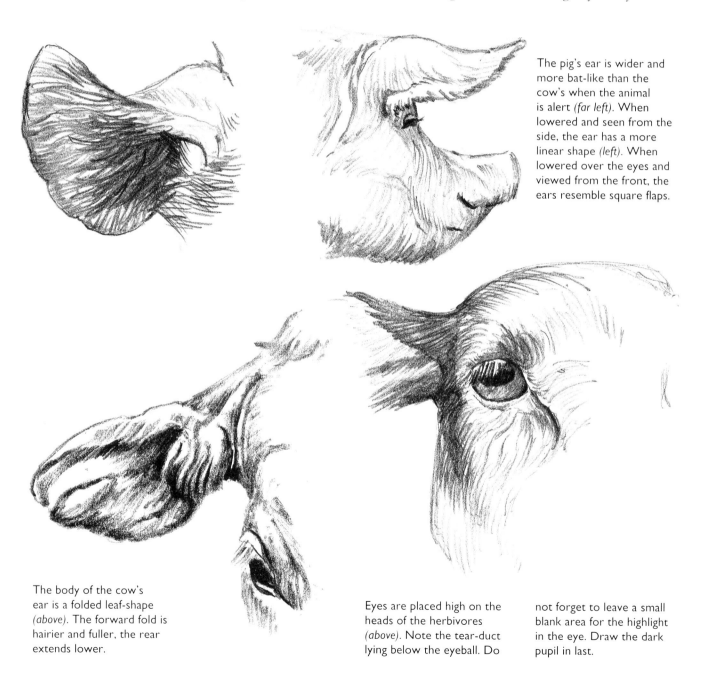

The pig's ear is wider and more bat-like than the cow's when the animal is alert *(far left)*. When lowered and seen from the side, the ear has a more linear shape *(left)*. When lowered over the eyes and viewed from the front, the ears resemble square flaps.

The body of the cow's ear is a folded leaf-shape *(above)*. The forward fold is hairier and fuller, the rear extends lower.

Eyes are placed high on the heads of the herbivores *(above)*. Note the tear-duct lying below the eyeball. Do not forget to leave a small blank area for the highlight in the eye. Draw the dark pupil in last.

The sheep's nose is more pointed than the cow's, and the nostrils are closer together, having

a narrower tear-drop shape *(above)*. The division in the middle of the upper lip is also more visible.

The pig's snout is made for rootling and pushing through soil and this is reflected in its shape *(above)*. The flat 'pushing'

end, which has almost an upside-down heart shape, is backed by circular folds of flesh that give the snout its flexibility.

1 The cow's muzzle is box-like and extends round into the fleshy upper jaw *(right)*. Two tear-drop shapes curling towards each other sum up the basis for the nostrils. They narrow into the rising 'V' on the bridge of the nose. Being a bulky animal, the cow can open its nostrils wider to inhale more air when it exerts itself.

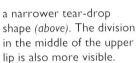

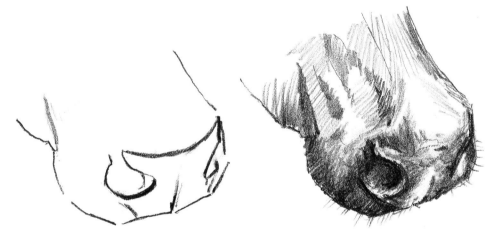

2 The cow's nose is damp and thus shiny, so remember to leave unmarked paper areas for highlights facing the light direction. The deeper tones inside the nostrils will need more pressure and a softer pencil.

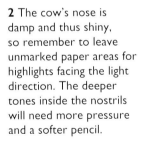

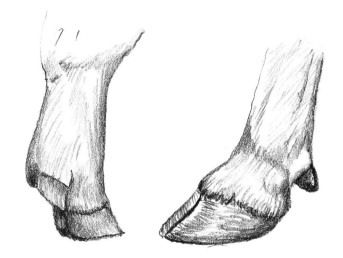

Pig's trotters lift the animal off the ground slightly *(far left)*. This gives the animal a springy walk.

The cow's cloven foot rests firmly on the ground *(left)*. As weight is put on to it, it splays somewhat. The redundant toes on both cows and pigs are placed up behind the foot, out of the way.

Farm birds

The red comb and wattles (the flap below the chin) are among the most familiar features of farmyard cockerels and hens, a signal to their companions of their relative health, and their status in the flock. The comb flares back from the beak, sometimes covering it; the wattles begin below the bill and extend past the eye, and the plumage flows from these down the nape and neck. The heads and eyes of these birds are not large – the eye is emphasized by a number of fleshy rings around it.

The cockerel's legs and feet are powerful, and plated with scales. This protects them from thorns in scrub where they scratch and search for food. The three-toed arrangement acts like a spreading stand, enabling the bird to rest easily on one leg.

The duck has a similar arrangement of toes, but webbing has evolved between them. Ducks waddle on land, but on water they float easily, propelled by these paddles. The toes are thinner than those of the cockerel and hen.

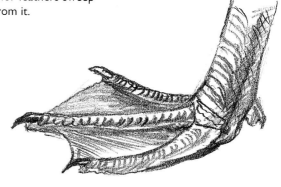
This chick has not grown adult features *(above)*. The eye appears nearer the bill, which is small.

Here *(above)* the artist has used a textured paper and soft pencil to work into the cockerel's comb. The pencil marks for feathers sweep back from it.

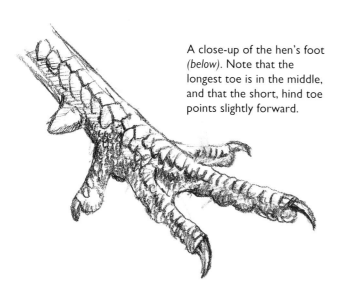

A close-up of the hen's foot *(below)*. Note that the longest toe is in the middle, and that the short, hind toe points slightly forward.

The duck's foot is similar in arrangement to the hen's, but the rear claw is undeveloped *(above)*.

Look for simple forms, such as triangles, rectangles and squares, as you draw the drake's tail *(right)*.

Feathers

Feather detail forms an important feature of farmyard birds. For example, the curly feathers that complete the rhythmic pattern of the drake's plumage have evolved from the upper tail coverts, supported by the tail. The tail itself is formed by overlapping, fan-like feathers.

In the case of the cockerel, the bird's 'sickles' are not tail feathers either but, like those of the drake, are highly evolved upper tail coverts which are supported by the tail itself. These sickles radiate out from the tail area, and wind and gravity twist and bend their shapes into visually exciting patterns.

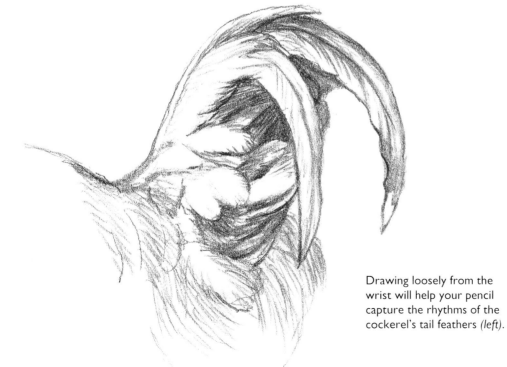

Drawing loosely from the wrist will help your pencil capture the rhythms of the cockerel's tail feathers *(left)*.

Artist's Tip

You do not always need to keep your pencils sharpened to a fine point. Use the bluntness of soft pencil work to convey the softness of feathers or fur.

Light and Shade

When you understand the principles of light and shade, your drawings of farm animals will become more convincingly three-dimensional.

When light falls on the animals' bodies, the parts nearest the light will be the brightest. As the light glances away, over and under the body, the surfaces become darker in tone. When the light is overhead, the darkest areas are under the body; when it comes from the side, both top and underneath will be deeper in tone.

Light direction
When you begin, observe your subject to see which direction the light is mainly coming from – bearing in mind that it may come from more than one direction.

The irregular surface of fur or feathers can, however, create complicated patterns of light and shade, but with practice you will soon learn to pick out the main masses that are highlighted or in shadow.

Although sketchy in quality, this drawing still conveys the broad masses of light and dark.

The massive shape of the bull *(right)* is a good subject for the study of shadow. I blocked out the main areas of light and shade, then hatched in pencil strokes for the middle tones and overlapped the strokes for the darkest. I left the upper areas untouched to suggest light on the form. The bull's head casts its own shadow on the neck.

Artist's Tip

Place a spherical object, such as an apple or orange, next to a direct light source, such as a table lamp, and study how the light affects it. You will find that the shadow often appears deepest where light and shade meet.

1 Draw in the outline of your hen lightly to suggest the main masses *(right)*.

2 Decide what direction the light is coming from – then begin to shade in these masses *(far right)*.

Texture and Pattern

As well as the differences in their overall shape, farm animals also have a variety of surface texture and pattern – think of the smooth, velvety quality of a horse's coat with its soft sheen, the matt, rough texture of sheep's wool, and the wonderful feather patterns and textures of hens and ducks.

Fur and feathers

All of these qualities can be expressed in different combinations of media and surface – the trick is to choose the combination which produces the quality you want most effectively.

The softness of sheep's wool might be conveyed by a medium that has a 'blurry' quality, such as charcoal, for example; the effect can be increased if this is used on a slightly rough surface. The bold stripes and patches on feathers could be well expressed by a medium that produces clean lines, such as pencil or felt-tip pen, applied to a relatively smooth surface.

The feather patterns of these turkeys *(above)* make a decorative pattern like a sunburst of marks radiating out from a centre. The wax crayon used makes a vital and decisive mark.

In this drawing of a sheep *(right)*, the artist has painted loosely on to rough watercolour paper and then worked over it with crayon and ink. He has deepened the background texture and allowed the sheep to emerge from it, keeping the white shafts of light on the wool clean.

In this drawing of a Tamworth pig *(left)*, the artist has used sweeping strokes of the pencil, on its side or its point, with varying pressure, to convey the coarse hairiness of the animal's coat.

Working in detail

Rough paper and the texture of charcoal pencil or chalk can be the means to make close studies of widely diverse animals.

In the study of a bull's head below, the overall rough texture suggests the animal's craggy form, and this overall quality unifies the details. The artist has carefully rendered the curly forelock, the fine hair around the nostrils, and the skin texture of the muzzle. He has held back from working too heavily into the forehead and nasal bridge to preserve their light tone. The horns are shiny with a line of highlight along them. The ears are hairy and dark and thus absorb light.

Another interesting alternative when conveying texture and pattern is to draw 'in reverse' using a light medium that is capable of making marks on a dark background. In the drawing opposite, the soft pastel has captured the patterns and highlights of the turkey's glossy feather masses.

Here *(right)* the artist has been sensitive to the different textures of skin and hair, and has varied the use of his pencil accordingly.

Artist's Tip

Always have a range of papers, colours and surfaces available so that you can try out different media on them to see what textures they produce.

This drawing has been produced in white pastel on black sugar paper *(right)*. The image could first be sketched out in a darker medium such as pencil.

Behaviour and Movement

Most farm animals live in herds or flocks; they are social and do things together. Although they are social creatures, this does not mean that they all have the same status. For example, a single cockerel will be dominant in the poultry flock, and his favourite hen will dominate the other hens – a position often ruthlessly maintained.

Maternal behaviour

To counteract this aggression, the relationship between parent and offspring is a touching sight that immediately appeals to the artist, as in the drawing of the long-legged foal feeding from its mother opposite.

The 'broody' mother hen is a particularly powerful symbol of maternal care. When she broods her chicks, she keeps them on her brood patch, fluffing out her feathers over them. They will shelter under her at night, or run to her in the day. As she feeds, she will keep an eye on them, over her shoulder.

Feeding habits

Knowing something of cows' biology will help you understand their behaviour. When they lie down to 'ruminate', for example, they are re-chewing the grass they have cropped in order to digest it.

In their various activities, cows tend to gather together, lying down for shade or rest. Here a small group of cows ruminates. I did this study in dilute Indian ink and a no. 4 brush which gives a nice point.

Artist's Tip

When you are observing animal behaviour, approach the animals gently and without noise. They will become less afraid and more inquisitive if you avoid eye-contact.

Observation and knowledge of light and shadow can help you put down an image quickly. Here *(above)* a Suffolk Punch foal feeds from its mother.

I had a photograph of some chicks which helped me visualize this image *(right)* which I had seen many times without actually drawing the scene.

The cockerel advertises its presence by crowing loudly *(left)*. The effort involved forces the cockerel to stretch its body, curve its neck and open its beak.

Soft pencil on cartridge paper is the best way to capture the quick movements of preening birds *(above)*. The feathers spread like petals from a flower.

Artist's Tip

Sometimes rapid movement defeats the eye. A mark or two and a squiggle can be built up later from your knowledge of the animals' forms.

Although the head has disappeared, the small feathers and the direction of feet give clues to this preening hen's pose *(above)*.

Geese are good sentinels *(left)*; they make cackling calls and hissing noises when alarmed. This is accompanied by the exciting serpentine shapes of their threat postures.

Animals in motion

The commotion illustrated below can happen suddenly; the piglets may be feeding quietly and then take it into their heads to stampede. When they run, their front and back legs stretch apart and close together in unison. When walking, the legs on one side close up, while on the other side they spread apart so that a sort of tripod effect constantly supports the body.

The panicking hens have lowered their heads, and the stretched angle of the legs is exaggerated. The feet appear to have left the ground because the shadow has been sketched in a few strokes below them.

The few static items – straw, pitchfork, and brickwork – provide a striking contrast that serves to emphasize the animals' movement.

A rich black wax pencil was used here. I sketched and traced out the drawing many times before I was satisfied with the composition.

Sketching

Sketching is the lifeblood of the animal artist's work. The pencil on the page will follow your watchful eye as it observes what is going on in the farmyard. Noting what you see will add to your growing store of information for more ambitious work such as painting and sculpture.

Making a start
Where do you begin? First, get yourself a sketchbook – the hardback type with paper that can take a wash of paint for colour-notes – and a soft pencil that will move swiftly and easily over the paper. Thus equipped, start by making mental notes on the animals and the general activity. Then, when you are ready, choose a particular subject to draw, and work fast; don't worry in the least if your sketch doesn't look 'right' – you can expand it when you get home.

As time goes on, your sketches will improve, and you will possess your own library, chock-full of all the animals you have recorded.

A sketch, improved at home, of two significant positions in feeding cows *(left)*. The cows make simple rectangular shapes.

The effect of light and shade, captured with charcoal on cartridge paper – a sketch which will make a good basis for a more finished composition later *(right)*. The dark background highlights the cow.

The artist looked for the simplest shapes when drawing these cows (above).

Bold pencil strokes, at different angles, convey the roughness of this Jacob's sheep's fleece (below).

The folded limbs and relaxed attitude of this bullock suggest peaceful rumination (above).

Any line was better than none as I tried to capture the feeling of massiveness in this bull's head and neck (above and above right).

Artist's Tip

Do not get too anxious when you begin sketching. Relax, take in the atmosphere and observe the animals before you start.

Visual reminder

Sketching is a means to aid your memory – what pigs' ears look like from diverse angles, the arch of a crowing cock's neck, or lambs climbing on their feeder. Your sketchbook is private, for your eyes only. It does not matter if your note is just a squiggle: it may be just what you need later for a detailed drawing or composition.

The important thing is to note your observation as soon as possible. Constant practice means improvement. You will find that your visual memory improves and you remember much more than you actually draw.

Suitable materials

You can sketch with a pencil, ballpoint, or felt-tip – whatever you feel at home with. You can take with you large pieces of paper on a board, a tiny notepad and clutch-pencil tucked in your top pocket, or a combination of them all.

The positions of the hens' feet fascinated me *(above* and *right)*, as did the shapes of the birds themselves.

These sketches of pigs' heads *(left, above* and *below)* are no more than a few lines, yet contain essential information. The full figure *(right)* records the form and markings.

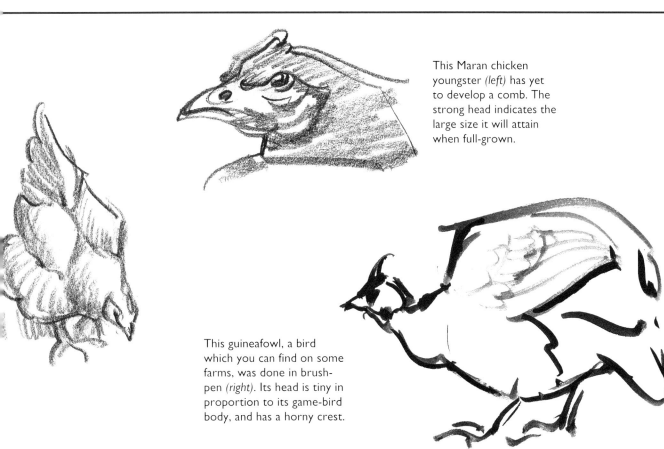

This Maran chicken youngster *(left)* has yet to develop a comb. The strong head indicates the large size it will attain when full-grown.

This guineafowl, a bird which you can find on some farms, was done in brush-pen *(right)*. Its head is tiny in proportion to its game-bird body, and has a horny crest.

Artist's Tip

Attract poultry with a handful of grain. They move quickly, but all your squiggles will capture movement and add to your knowledge.

Using pencil and wash, the artist here has noted the bow-shaped resting cockerel, and the upright tails of the chickens *(left)*.

In Setting

When placing your farmyard animals in a setting, it is always tempting to include too much surrounding paraphenalia – but avoid this temptation. A mass of details can distract from the animal or bird which is your main subject.

Setting the scene

Think of the scene as a stage setting, in which just a few clues may be enough to create a sense of place. A single bucket or fence-post, for example, will convey a farmyard setting.

In this drawing, I varied the tones and the weight of line to separate the various elements that make up the whole. Notice, for example, how I used a dark line along the sow's back to separate her from the fence, and visually to bring her body forwards in the space.

Choosing what to include

When creating a setting, try to include only 'working' details that provide useful information and contribute to the composition. In the drawing below, the perspective of the bars on the gate as they spread out towards us tells us that we are looking down on the animals, while implying space in the foreground in which they can move about – piglets are always restless. A few pencil marks on the ground suggest wisps of straw, in contrast to the bold uprights of the fence which are strong enough to contain the sow's bulk.

The drinking basin in the foreground echoes the sow's shape, and draws the eye in. Including such authentic details shows that the artist has looked carefully at the scene.

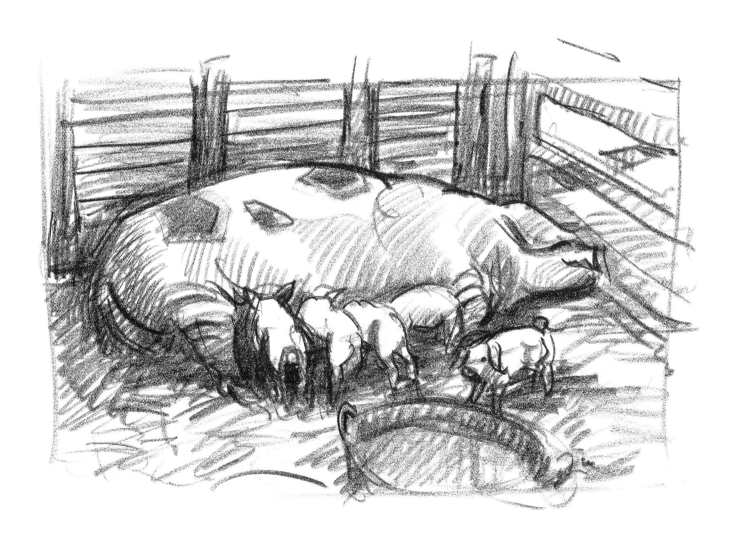

Mood and time

As well as giving a sense of physical place, situating an animal in a setting can also be a way of conveying a particular mood, time, or event. For example, including just a simple shadow may be enough to suggest light direction, time of day, and weather conditions.

Drawings of mother animals with their young create a powerful sense of place and time, and may need little additional detail. In the two drawings on this page, the only hint of physical surroundings are a few wispy lines to suggest straw and shadow.

Here *(above)*, the artist has captured the relationship between mother and calf – both shapes echo each other. Interest is provided by the textures of hair and straw, drawn with a clutch pencil. This gives a fine line without the need for constant sharpening.

I used a soft 8B pencil to produce these sketches of a ewe and her lamb *(right)*. The lamb had just been born and lay prone for a while, but within an hour it was tottering around after its mother.

I was careful not to disturb these ducks *(left)* and was thus able to capture their sleeping forms snuggled into the grass, which is suggested by a few sketchy lines.

Working from sketches
All the close-up studies of farm birds on this page began life as notes put down speedily for later information.

Adding small authentic items such as drinking and food bowls around which the animals gather can build a sketch up into a scene. Larger areas such as stables, or even the farms where animals are gathered for exhibition and competition, provide a fascinating backdrop for your animals.

The Aylesbury ducks on the left are enjoying a rest on the grass, their two bodies echoing each other. Below left, two bantams work around a feeder. Below right, the hen with her chicks looks relaxed and safe amongst the straw, while the chick shares the food with its mother. The small, intimate details in such drawings do much to convey a sense of mood and setting.

A quick sketch of two hens pecking at a feeder *(above)* conjures in the mind a much wider farmyard scene.

This sketch was done with a clutch-type pencil – the artist strengthened the drawing later *(above)*.

This sketch of feeding time for the huge Suffolk Punch horses *(above)* was done on the spot. I added to it later.

Agricultural shows provide excellent opportunities for gathering information. This quick pencil study of people and animals *(right)* was done at one such show, where some fine examples were being judged.

Framing and Composition

Framing refers to the size and proportions of the paper or surface you choose to work within. You do not need to accept the sizes provided by the manufacturers. You can select any section from your picture, vertical or horizontal. It may vastly improve your composition.

Composition is about arranging the elements you want to use in your picture to maximum effect. It may take some thought and many small sketches to decide what will work best. You will be looking to create mood, atmosphere and meaning.

Deciding on a composition
When you get down to the design, ask yourself what person, animal or thing is most important to the picture and how you can bring this out.

You may find that you have – reluctantly – to leave out some favourite item that does not contribute to the main theme. Never mind; this can start off a new picture!

Try out different media in your preparatory drawings, too. Does the subject suggest charcoal, or pencil? Does it demand pen and ink, or coloured wax pencils?

Two examples
In the light-hearted composition of sheep blocking a country lane here, I have tackled the scene from two angles – one a low viewpoint, the other higher. In the smaller sketch, the shepherd's figure is larger. This could be further enhanced by framing down – reducing the area around him, even cropping out part of the car.

This is a working sketch, much rubbed out, altered and re-drawn. The sketches of the little car were done at a rally. Soft pencil is the quickest means of doing thumbnail sketches.

Scale and balance

In the first small sketch, the figure and car dominate the scene – they are bigger and the light falls behind them. The sheep are about to surround the viewer. In the second, larger drawing, I have allowed space for the sheep to move into. The shepherd emerges from the shady lane into the light, and the car is almost concealed, only to be noticed later.

Remember to keep your composition simple. Avoid placing your important figures slap in the middle; place them to the side and above the middle to avoid predictability.

This piece was done on tinted paper with pen and wash. A little white was added for highlights on the foliage. It is always best to work lightly to begin with and steadily deepen lines and tones as necessary.

Artist's Tip

As you work across your drawing adding tone and detail, use a piece of paper under your hand to avoid greasing or smudging work you have already done.

Working from Photographs

Artists have always made use of photographs, and film and video can provide the animal artist with more information than ever before.

Using the camera
I always carry a still camera with me on my trips, but use it mostly for recording background detail: I never rely on the camera entirely and always sketch as well. Photographs offer us only one small moment in time, whereas sketches can capture movement, space and continuity, as our eyes scan the whole scene.

If you want to sketch in comfort, television films and programmes, recorded on video, provide the ideal opportunity. Although both camera and animal move, the freeze-frame facility will allow you to stop the film to do your drawing.

Highland cattle have a distinctive appearance, but are not that easy to find, so a photograph *(above)* provides a useful reference. I began by doing a fairly literal copy of the photograph *(above right)*, paying particular attention to areas of light and shade.

In my second attempt, I focused on one area of the animal around the head and shoulder *(right)*. Fading out at the edges, the drawing makes a pleasing arrangement, no longer confined by the rectangle of the original image.

66

A starting point

We do not have to be slaves to the photograph: it can be a departure point for a range of approaches. You can, for example, combine images from different photographs in one composition. Alternatively, if the arrangement of items in the photograph doesn't work as well as it might, you can always leave out, or add, a particular element when doing your drawing.

Remember, a photograph or video picture is merely a visual aid. Avoid copying it slavishly, and your drawing will be much more lively.

To achieve my final drawing, I used the animal from the photograph, but built in other elements to add interest and balance to the composition – there are now two Highland cattle grazing in a field, with a line of trees behind. Note the interplay of light and dark areas, and how these make the drawing easier to 'read'.

Horses

David Brown

Choosing the Right Medium

I

2

Mention the word 'drawing' and the majority of people will immediately think of a pencil drawing, for the humble pencil is probably the most popular of all drawing tools. There are three reasons for this. First is the pencil's convenience – it is light, small, and therefore easy to carry about. Second, it is relatively clean to use compared with charcoal, pastel, or pen and ink. And finally, it is cheap and easily obtainable in stationery and art shops.

In spite of these obvious advantages, I would urge you to experiment by trying out as many different media as possible: only by doing this will you discover the distinctive quality of each. There will come a time when you will need to know what medium to use to help you to produce a drawing with a specific effect. Knowing the various media, and the differences between them, will help you to choose the one most likely to produce the effect you want.

As well as the tool you use, you will need to think about the surface you are going to work on, for this, too, will affect the final 'look' of your work. Experiment with different media on different surfaces, to see how various combinations work together.

In the pictures on these two pages, I have produced six drawings of the same horse's head to illustrate how much its appearance changes with each change of medium and surface.

I Technical pen on smooth paper
2 Felt-tip pen on rough paper
3 Watercolour on rough watercolour paper
4 Pastel pencil on coloured Ingres paper
5 HB pencil on 'not' paper
6 Dip pen and Indian ink on smooth cartridge

3

5

4

6

Proportion and Measuring

An essential part of producing a good drawing lies in getting the basics right. For many people proportion presents one of the biggest challenges, yet it is of utmost importance to achieve the correct proportions if you want your drawing to look convincing. Whether your chosen subject be an animal, a human, a plant or a building, if the basic structure is wrong, you will not be able to put things right by your use of shading or colour.

The pencil method

A simple method of discovering the correct proportions of your subject is illustrated below. Choose a certain part of your subject and use this as your *measuring unit*. Hold your pencil at arm's length and line up the top of it with the top of the measuring unit – in this instance the horse's head. Now place your thumb on the pencil in line with the bottom of the head. You now have a measuring unit with which to work out how many head lengths make up the length of the body; hold the pencil horizontally to find out how many make up the width.

When you are measuring like this, always keep your arm straight, your pencil vertical, and your thumb on the same spot on the pencil.

Judging by eye

You can test yourself to find out how good, or bad, you are at judging proportions without measuring them. Choose your subject: if you don't have a live horse to draw, you could use

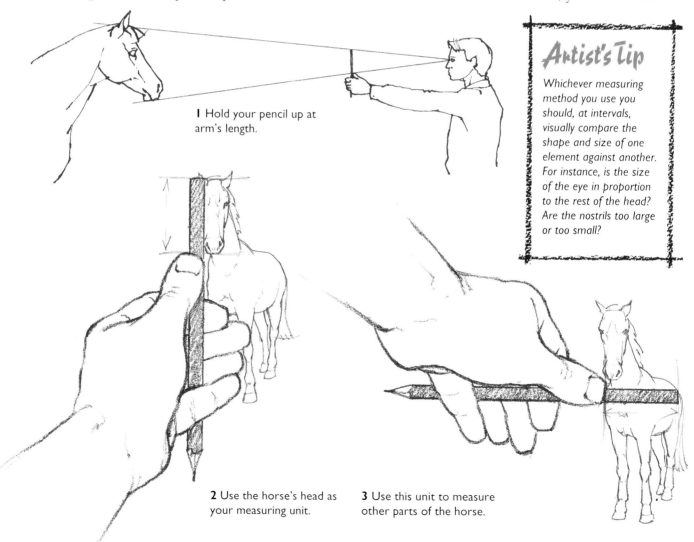

1 Hold your pencil up at arm's length.

2 Use the horse's head as your measuring unit.

3 Use this unit to measure other parts of the horse.

a photograph (a photograph may be better in this case because the subject won't move while you are doing your test!). It should be a good picture, though, and the larger, the better.

Now do a simple drawing of the horse. Don't bother with any details for this exercise – in fact, you need only put a series of marks on the paper to indicate the size of the head, how large you think the body should be, and how long the legs and other parts of the horse are in relation to the head.

Checking your drawing
To find out how accurate you are at judging proportions by eye, compare your drawing with the photograph. First check the proportions of the horse in the photograph by the 'pencil method' already described – although this doesn't have to be done at arm's length – and record the results.

Next, check the proportions of your drawing to see how well they accord with those of the horse in the photograph.

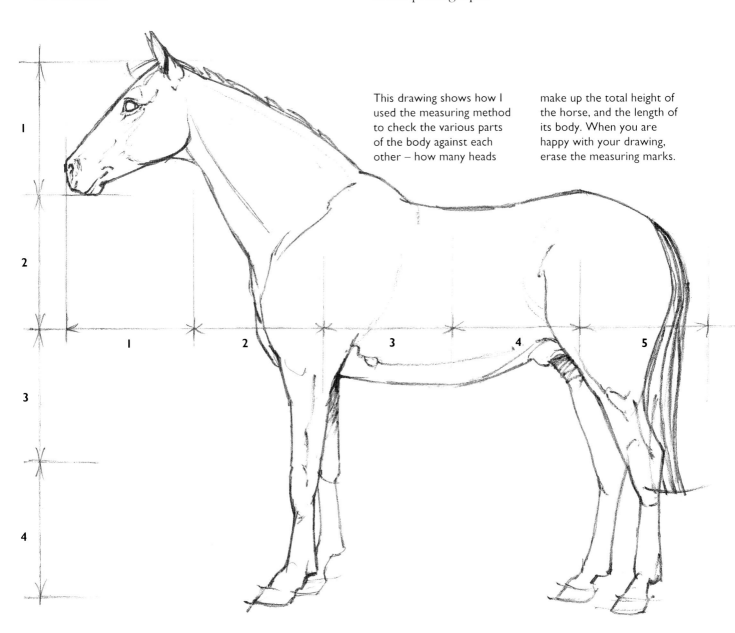

This drawing shows how I used the measuring method to check the various parts of the body against each other – how many heads make up the total height of the horse, and the length of its body. When you are happy with your drawing, erase the measuring marks.

Practice makes perfect

You should always use the pencil method of measuring when doing your basic drawing. With practice your eye and brain will become experienced enough to dispense with the technique, only using it to check your drawing if it looks wrong; until then, persevere with it. Remember, you must get the proportions and angles right when drawing your basic lines as these will be the foundations on which you will build up your drawing.

I To draw this head, I first roughly drew the outline shape. Then I drew a line from the top of the head to the point at which the head connects to the neck (A). This was to be my unit of measurement.

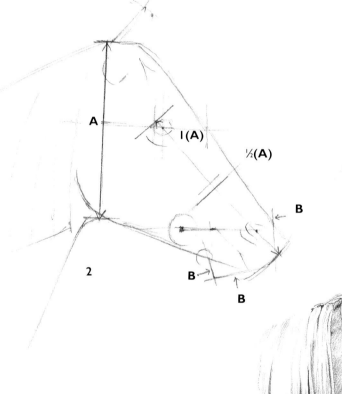

3 When I had compared and corrected all the proportions and marked in the position of key details, I was able to erase my construction lines, and work up the finished drawing.

2 I noticed that the position of the eye lined up to a point half-way down line A. The distance from the back of the eye to the end of the nose, line I(A), was the same as the length of line A, and half-way down this line gave me the position of the strap, at ½(A). I was able to compare measurements around the chin, mouth and nostril, using line B as my guide. By holding the pencil vertically, I worked out the angles in this area.

To increase your awareness of proportion, keep comparing the various sections visually as you work. For example, how does the length of the upper front leg compare to that of the back leg? How do these compare to the length of the head? How do the widths compare?

Close-up

A tethered horse gives you the opportunity to make a detailed drawing. First make a simple sketch of the shape of the head. Then take a distance between two points as a measure: for example, from the top of the head to the point where the head meets the neck – line A in the drawing on the far left. Use this as a measure to help you build up the rest of the head.

Checking the angles

In addition to checking that each part of your drawing is the correct size in relation to the others, you must also check that the angles are correct. This can be done by holding your pencil vertically in front of you so that it runs down the length of the horse. Move your eyes down the pencil, taking note of the position and angle of the various body parts in relation to the vertical line.

Using a plumbline

I remember being encouraged at art school to use a plumbline for checking angles. Making your own plumbline is a simple task: merely tie a small weight on the end of a piece of string or cotton. Then all you have to do is hold the end of the string, letting the weight hang free to give you a true vertical line. This method is more accurate than using a pencil, but it does have one disadvantage: you will need both hands to prevent the weight swinging from side to side as you move the plumbline from one part of the body to another.

A plumbline is easy to make, and helps you to check the vertical lines and angles in your subject.

Artist's Tip

Before embarking upon a study drawing make sure that you are comfortable – you may need to stay in that position for some time.

Structure and Form

In order to understand the surface shape of the horse, it is helpful to know something of its skeletal and muscular structure.

Bones and muscles

It isn't necessary to make a serious study of the horse's anatomy unless, of course, you intend to specialize professionally. But it is very helpful to carry out a limited study, making notes on how the structure of the bones – particularly those close to the surface – affects the surface shape. A general knowledge of the muscles which directly affect the surface would also be useful.

In this drawing of a horse's skeleton (above), the arrows show which bones most affect the outer form.

Studying these muscles (below) will help you to understand the surface shape of a horse.

Finding references

References for horse anatomy can be found in natural history museums, but it would be more convenient to check in your local library first. This may stock books on horse health and care, which would almost certainly contain illustrated diagrams which would be helpful to you.

Perspective

If you want your drawings of horses to look convincing, you'll also need to know something of the rules governing perspective. Perspective is an optical illusion which allows artists to represent three-dimensional objects on a flat, two-dimensional surface.

There are three forms of perspective: *linear, tonal* or *aerial*, and *foreshortening*. All three can be used to convey depth and distance. Knowing how they work is indispensable when constructing your three-dimensional drawing.

Linear perspective rules that objects decrease in size the further they are from the person viewing them. So a horse in the foreground of a picture will appear larger than a horse in the middle ground or distance – although, in reality, the two may be the same size.

Because of perspective, the hind quarters of the smaller horse *(below left)* hide its shoulders, and make its head appear smaller. In the larger horse *(below right)*, lines have been used to work out the angles.

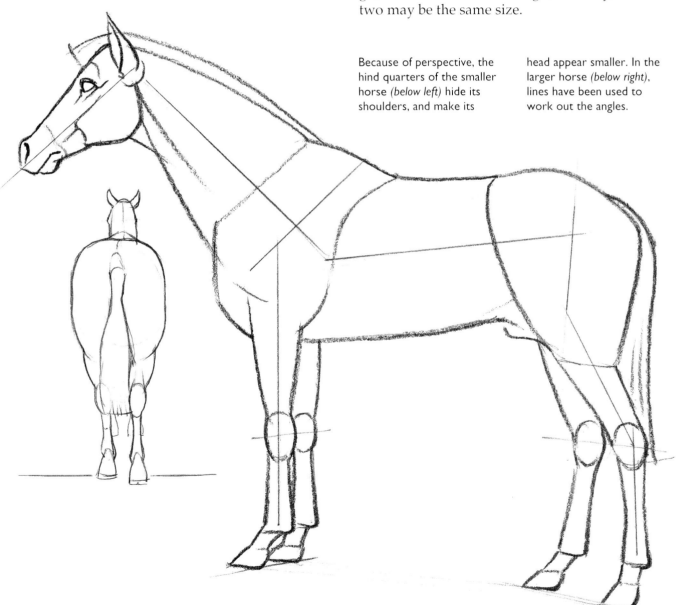

This drawing *(above)* illustrates the effects of both linear and tonal perspective. The horse on the left is clearly to the rear of the scene because it appears smaller. It is also paler in tone, conveying a sense of distance.

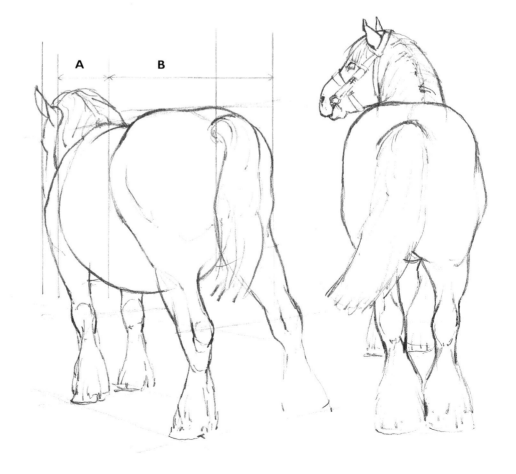

Drawing vertical lines down the various sections accentuates the foreshortening of this workhorse *(right)*. You can clearly see how small an area is taken up by the body (A), compared to the hind quarters (B). The foreshortening of the horse on the far right is so severe that the body has virtually disappeared.

Tonal perspective is an illusory effect that makes distant objects appear lighter in colour and outline than those nearer the observer. It is caused by atmospheric conditions which subdue colours and reduce the differences between light and shade. This will, of course, be hardly noticeable when viewing a horse, as one end would not be far enough away from the other to make any difference. You can use 'artist's licence', however, and exaggerate this illusion to help to convey depth and achieve a three-dimensional effect.

Foreshortening works in a similar way to linear perspective, except that it distorts the proportions in a single object, making the part nearest the viewer appear larger, and the part furthest away appear smaller. This makes it all the more important to use the measuring method described on pages 72–3 when working out the position and proportions of the various features and sections of the horse. You will be surprised at how small an area some of the body parts occupy when foreshortened.

Horses' legs

One area that is sure to cause the beginner problems is the lower part of the leg. However, with careful observation and repeated practice at drawing this part, you will soon be able to obtain creditable results.

The drawings on this page will, I hope, help you to understand the structure of the lower front leg. Drawing 1 is a front view of a horse's right leg. Notice the slight angle through the ankle and knee joints (on the left leg, of course, they would slope in the other direction. Hold the drawing in front of a mirror to see this).

Compare drawings 1 and 3 (a side view of a leg) to the two simplified drawings 2 and 4. You will notice that in drawing 2 the leg is virtually the same width across the B and C lines, narrowing slightly between the two, whereas when looked at from the side, in drawing 4, the leg becomes wider as it descends to the ankle.

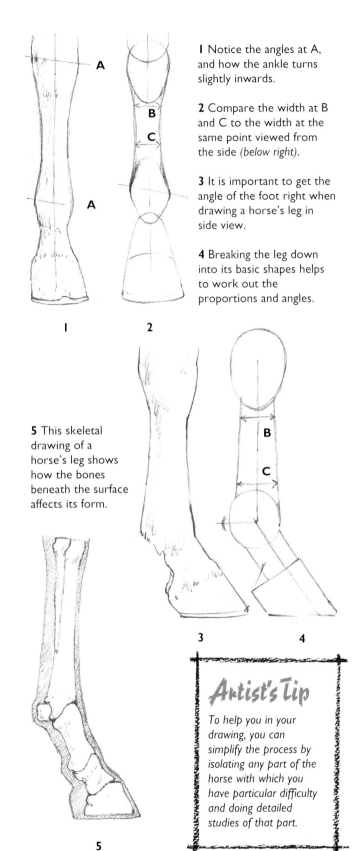

1 Notice the angles at A, and how the ankle turns slightly inwards.

2 Compare the width at B and C to the width at the same point viewed from the side *(below right)*.

3 It is important to get the angle of the foot right when drawing a horse's leg in side view.

4 Breaking the leg down into its basic shapes helps to work out the proportions and angles.

5 This skeletal drawing of a horse's leg shows how the bones beneath the surface affects its form.

Artist's Tip

To help you in your drawing, you can simplify the process by isolating any part of the horse with which you have particular difficulty and doing detailed studies of that part.

Looking at Features

Horses' heads are full of intricate shapes and are fascinating to draw. To understand how these shapes work, do as many drawings as you can, perhaps keeping them all in one sketchbook for convenience, which you can then refer back to when you are unsure of some detail. In this way, you will build up knowledge which in time will enable you to produce drawings without having to check references.

Artist's Tip

Before beginning a drawing, take some time to walk around your subject. It will enable you to get a better feel of the three-dimensional shape and bulk of the horse, and this will help you in the construction of your drawing.

Here *(above* and *left)* you can see the advantage of drawing from different viewpoints. It would be very difficult to visualize what the front view of the head would look like merely by studying the head in profile.

Features

A horse's head is essentially an elongated cube, constructed from various different features and forms. When you do your drawing, observe how the different features relate to each other – how one form flows into or moulds itself around the next – and how the forms all fit together into the overall structure of the head.

Study the eye carefully; what shape are the eyelids and how do they relate to the eye? How do the eyes fit into the head? How do they relate to the position of the ears and what area of the head do they occupy?

Now look at the shape of the nostrils, and the proportion of the area they take up. How far does the mouth extend up the side of the head?

Changing viewpoints
As you shift your viewpoint, so the features and forms in a horse's head shift in shape and angle, too. To get a feeling for these changes, study the head from a variety of positions – for example, do a side view, then a view from the front, then a three-quarter view. Notice how the shape of the nostrils changes, also the eyes. Look at the changing shape of the ears. Make detailed drawings of all of these different parts from various viewpoints.

This profile *(above)* is a similar view to the one below, but I did not draw it from so extreme an angle. Compare the position and shape of the eye and nostril with those in the other drawings on these two pages.

This three-quarter view *(left)* has a more three-dimensional feeling because it is seen from behind, so that the underneath as well as the side of the head is visible.

Ears

Although they appear simple at first glance, ears are really quite complex when studied in detail. Many people experience difficulty in placing the ears in the right position on the head.

To help you to overcome this difficulty, add a little of the surrounding area when doing your drawing, making a graphic note on how the ears relate to, say, the position and angles of the eyes. This can be done by adding lines as shown in the drawing below. You can clearly see how, in this particular pose, the lines fanning out from the ear relate to the lines of the eye and neck. Look carefully, too, at how the ears 'grow' out of the head.

The angle and shape of the ears does change, of course, depending on what the horse is doing. A horse will twist its ears around and back if it is interested in some sound from behind – and if sounds come from several directions at once, the horse may simultaneously have one ear angled forward and the other back!

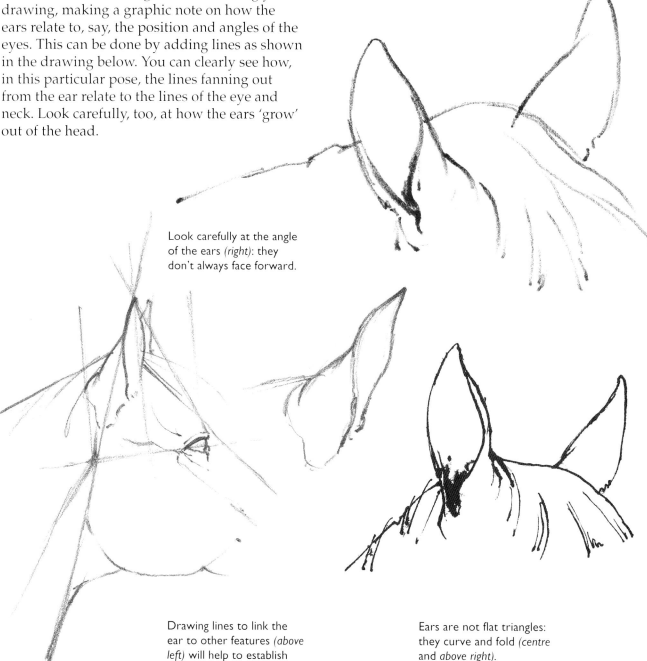

Look carefully at the angle of the ears *(right)*: they don't always face forward.

Drawing lines to link the ear to other features *(above left)* will help to establish their position.

Ears are not flat triangles: they curve and fold *(centre and above right)*.

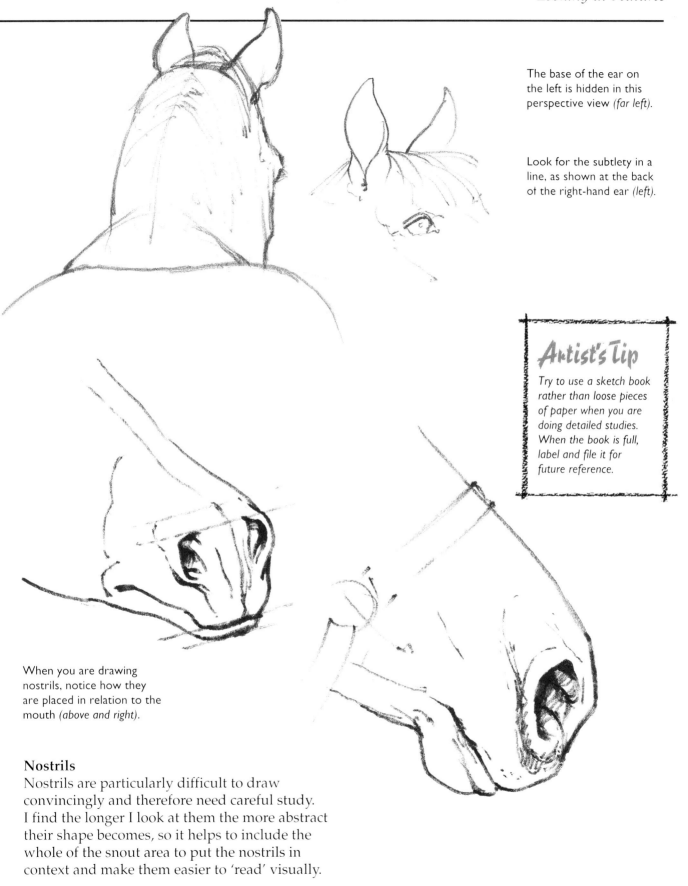

The base of the ear on the left is hidden in this perspective view *(far left)*.

Look for the subtlety in a line, as shown at the back of the right-hand ear *(left)*.

When you are drawing nostrils, notice how they are placed in relation to the mouth *(above and right)*.

Nostrils

Nostrils are particularly difficult to draw convincingly and therefore need careful study. I find the longer I look at them the more abstract their shape becomes, so it helps to include the whole of the snout area to put the nostrils in context and make them easier to 'read' visually.

Different Breeds

There are many different breeds of horse, each with its own distinctive characteristics of shape, size and proportion. You could study the differences between the various breeds by finding references for as many of them as possible, and making careful drawings of each.

As you build up your study collection, take note of what it is that makes one breed different from another; there is more than size that separates a sturdy Shetland pony from a hunter, for example. Consider age differences, too: a foal has very different proportions to those of its mother.

Workhorses and thoroughbred horses

The most obvious difference is that between a workhorse and a thoroughbred. Leg length is probably the most striking distinction here. Although both types have fairly bulky bodies, the legs of thoroughbreds are long and slender in proportion to their bodies, while those of workhorses are much shorter. Workhorses have a much stockier build altogether.

This drawing of a racehorse *(above)*, done in conté crayon, shows its characteristic length of leg. Notice the fluid, backward sweep of its hind legs.

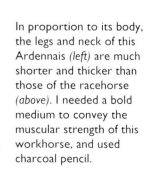

In proportion to its body, the legs and neck of this Ardennais *(left)* are much shorter and thicker than those of the racehorse *(above)*. I needed a bold medium to convey the muscular strength of this workhorse, and used charcoal pencil.

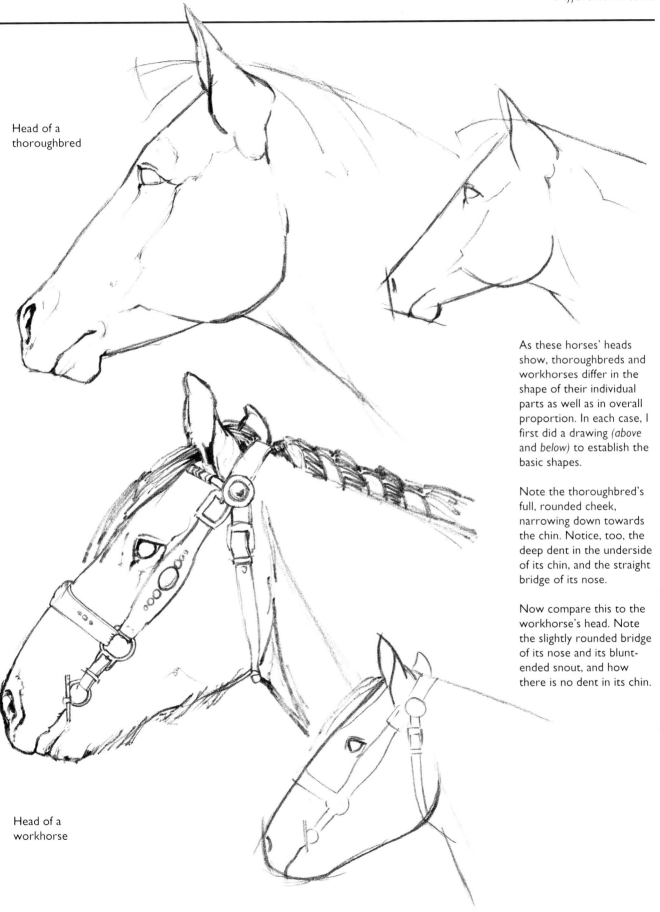

Head of a
thoroughbred

Head of a
workhorse

As these horses' heads
show, thoroughbreds and
workhorses differ in the
shape of their individual
parts as well as in overall
proportion. In each case, I
first did a drawing *(above
and below)* to establish the
basic shapes.

Note the thoroughbred's
full, rounded cheek,
narrowing down towards
the chin. Notice, too, the
deep dent in the underside
of its chin, and the straight
bridge of its nose.

Now compare this to the
workhorse's head. Note
the slightly rounded bridge
of its nose and its blunt-
ended snout, and how
there is no dent in its chin.

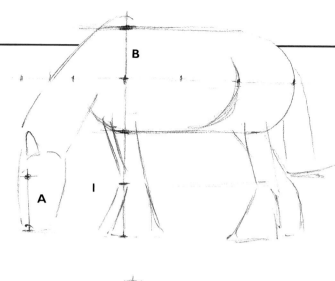

Workhorse breeds

Although workhorses are all generally heavy in build, there are distinctions even within this one category that mark one breed from another.

A workhorse's size, proportions and shape reflect the work it was bred to do. The Shetland, shown opposite, is a very small horse which originates from the Shetland Isles, where it was used for carrying peat and generally pulling carts. Because of the harsh climate of the Islands, it developed a thick coat and a long, thick mane and tail as protection against the weather.

The larger Clydesdale, shown on this page, was used successfully for haulage work at the coalfields, as well as heavy agricultural work.

Comparing size

Size is probably the most obvious difference between the breeds – to realize how great the range is, just compare a diminutive Shetland pony to an enormous Shire horse!

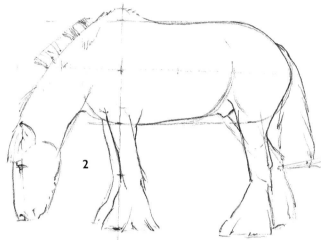

1 I drew this Clydesdale with a 2B pencil on medium-rough CS2 'not' paper. Using the length from eye to nostril (A) gave me a handy measuring unit, allowing me to work out the proportions quickly. Drawing a vertical line down through the shoulder (B) showed the backward slant of the legs.

2 When I was satisfied with the proportions of the basic shapes, I began to refine the drawing, adding more detail and erasing unwanted guide lines.

3 Finally, I completed the details and added shading to indicate the three-dimensional shape of the horse.

1

2

Comparing proportions

Proportions vary from one breed to another, too. For example, the proportions of the Clydesdale opposite are not dissimilar to those of the thoroughbred – although much heavier in build, *in proportion* its head is similarly small, and its neck and legs similarly long. By comparison with the Clydesdale, the little Shetland's head is relatively big and its legs relatively short.

Artist's Tip

The chinagraph pencil used for the Shetland pony on this page is almost impossible to erase so, if using chinagraph, do your basic drawing in soft pencil first.

1 To draw this Shetland pony, I first used a soft pencil to rough out the basic shape.

2 I then worked over the lines with a chinagraph pencil, adding details and erasing unwanted lines.

3 The final stage was to add a watercolour wash for the coloured areas.

3

Light and Shade

Without light and shade, a drawing may remain just an outline shape, with no sense of three-dimensional form – as you can clearly see in the two diagrams below. Without shading, the ball on the left is just a circle, floating in space; add shading and it is instantly transformed into a three-dimensional sphere.

Experimenting with light

To understand the principles of light and shade, try to spend some time studying the effect light has on an object. The object you choose for your study could be anything but, to start with, a simple, rounded shape, such as a ball or round fruit, would be best.

Natural light cannot be controlled in the same way as artificial light, so do your experimenting indoors, initially using just a single table lamp or torch to avoid complicated shadows. Try moving the light around to different locations around the object, placing it close and then further away to see how this affects the *modelling* – creating three-dimensional form with shading.

Highlights and shadows

As well as giving a flat object three-dimensional form, light and shade also help to show where an object curves outwards and where it hollows. Essentially, light will *highlight* raised or prominent shapes facing the light. Sunken areas, on the side away from the light, will be in shadow.

Reflected light

By careful observation you will discover that light can behave in an unexpected way. For example, the area most hidden from the light source is not necessarily the darkest. This is because light may be reflected back on to the subject matter from surrounding surfaces, producing shadows of varying degrees of intensity. Within these shadows there may be lighter patches, or *low lights*.

Light may, of course, also come from more than just a single source, although this one source may be more powerful than others.

Variations in tone

Modelling a drawing of a horse is a perfect example of these subtleties in light and shade. Unlike a simple rounded ball or orange, a horse is a complicated shape, made up of a whole series of different curves and hollows.

To work out where the highlights, low lights and shadows fall, it helps to break your subject down into more basic forms. You will find many tones between the lightest and darkest areas, but you can simplify the exercise by just using, say, two or three tones: a dark one for the darkest areas, a mid-grey for the middle tones and white paper for those areas directly facing the light.

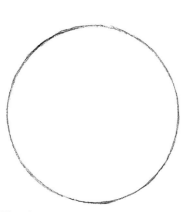

This drawing is no more than an empty circle, with no three-dimensional form.

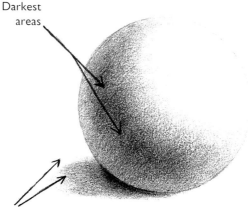

Light source

Darkest areas

Reflected light

The same drawing, with the addition of shading, instantly becomes a solid-looking ball.

Artist's Tip

If your subject is not affected by reflected light, cheat – and add your own light to create an even more three-dimensional effect.

1 Here, the arrows coming from the top left indicate the light source, and the arrows in the opposite direction the reflected light. Note how I broke down the head into basic shapes to help me work out the variations in light and shade.

2 Using my previous study drawing as a guide, I used soft pencil to produce this drawing of a horse's head, modelled in light and shade.

Changing light

If you are working in natural light – say, doing a sketch of a horse out-of-doors – bear in mind that the strength and direction of the light will change as time passes, and this will affect the intensity of the highlights and where the shadows fall. So that you don't have to keep amending your work, you might like, after drawing in your basic shapes, to make a mental note of the direction of the light source and lightly block in the shaded side as a reminder.

Cast shadows

Light also causes an object to cast shadows on to other objects or surfaces. This can become complicated if for some reason the light is coming from two or more different sources. When this happens, one light could cancel out part, or all, of the shadow cast by the other light, as illustrated in the diagrams below. Make sure, therefore, when you are drawing specifically to study shadows, that the light comes from one source only.

Shapes and angles

Look carefully at the angle at which the shadow falls in relation to the direction from which the light is coming.

Look also at the shape of the shadow. A shadow is never exactly the same shape as the object casting it, but a distorted version. The position of the light source will affect the length of a shadow: for example, a sun high in the sky will create short shadows, while a low sun creates elongated ones.

The surface on which a shadow falls also changes its outline. A relatively even surface, such as a wooden floor, will produce a fairly smooth outline; a rough surface, such as grass or stony ground, will break up a shadow, producing a jagged, patchy shape.

Artist's Tip

If your subject appears to be floating in space, 'anchor' it to the surface on which it is sitting or standing by adding a little shading underneath.

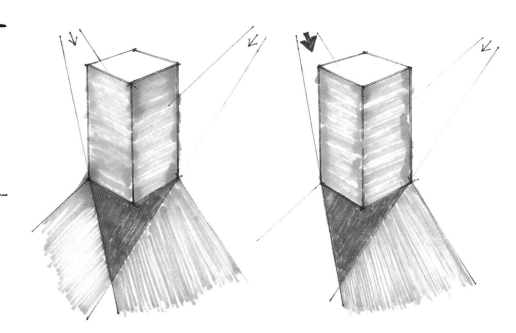

I did this drawing of a foal *(opposite)* on Ingres paper, using conté crayon. Here, the light is coming from above and slightly to the left, creating shadow on the right and underneath the animal. Although the shadow on the ground does not strongly echo the foal's shape, notice how important it is in linking the animal firmly to the surface.

These two diagrams show the possible effects of light from two different sources. In the diagram on the left, both lights are of equal strength and soften part of the shadow cast by each other. Only the central shadow, which neither light can reach, remains dark.

In the second diagram, the light on the left is stronger and obliterates part of the shadow cast by the light on the right.

Behaviour and Expression

On the whole, horses are very sedate creatures – one has only to observe the control a small girl has on an animal that dwarfs her in size, weight and strength to realize this. Nevertheless, there are times when horses show emotion, ranging from tenderness through to sheer joy and excitement.

While out walking one day I saw an owner release his horse into a small field. The horse immediately took off and galloped around the field for a while and then got down and proceeded to roll back and forth on its back. You could clearly see the exuberant sense of liberation felt by the animal.

Photographic reference

Trying to sketch such animated action accurately would pose a severe challenge for even the most experienced artist, and this is where a camera can be invaluable. If you take a few quick shots, capturing as many different angles and movements as possible, you can then use the ones you prefer as reference for drawings. Don't dispose of the other ones – a good supply of photographic reference is an essential part of any artist's kit and you may one day want to draw the same behaviour from another angle.

Odd angles

Although a photograph will accurately show the position of the body, head and limbs you may still find it hard to draw such a pose convincingly. The viewer's eye is accustomed to the normal stance of a horse and will question an unusual viewpoint. However, if you practise drawing horses from different perspectives you will become more familiar with the whole shape of the horse and more confident in portraying such 'quirky' poses.

I used charcoal pencil to capture this fleeting moment – a profile of a horse neighing.

Artist's Tip

When working from photographs, don't allow yourself to get bogged down with minor details. Imagine that the animal depicted will move in the next few minutes so that you have to work quickly to draw the basic shape, just as if you were working from life.

When you are drawing horses in motion, use a free-flowing medium that will allow you to produce a loose, fluid line that will convey a sense of movement. Even when drawing from photographs, work quickly. For these two rolling horses (*above* and *below*), I chose a broad, chisel pencil.

Horses grazing

If you prefer to start with something less challenging than a horse rolling about on the ground, a horse in the process of eating – whether from a trough or bag, or grazing – would be a good choice. An animal feeding from some form of container would be ideal because, apart from the head, there would be little or no movement in the body. This would give you time to choose your viewpoint and either do one carefully measured drawing, putting in as much detail as possible, or two or three quick sketches from different angles.

There is more movement in a grazing horse, but it is very slight, giving you an excellent opportunity to do a series of sketching studies.

Flexible medium

Because of its flexibility, watercolour is an excellent medium to choose for depicting horse behaviour. It is a medium which I enjoy using a great deal, and has an aesthetic quality which I like very much. You can be very exact with it, keeping it tight to produce realistic, detailed work, or use it loosely to produce fresh, free-flowing work. I have also used it in combination with coloured pencils to sharpen up the details on a drawing.

This horse was drawn from a photograph, using watercolour. I first lightly drew the shape, putting in just the bare amount of information I needed: I didn't want to overwork the drawing because I wanted the freedom to draw with the brush as I painted. Although I had plenty of time because I was drawing from a photograph, I worked quickly as if I expected the animal to move at any moment.

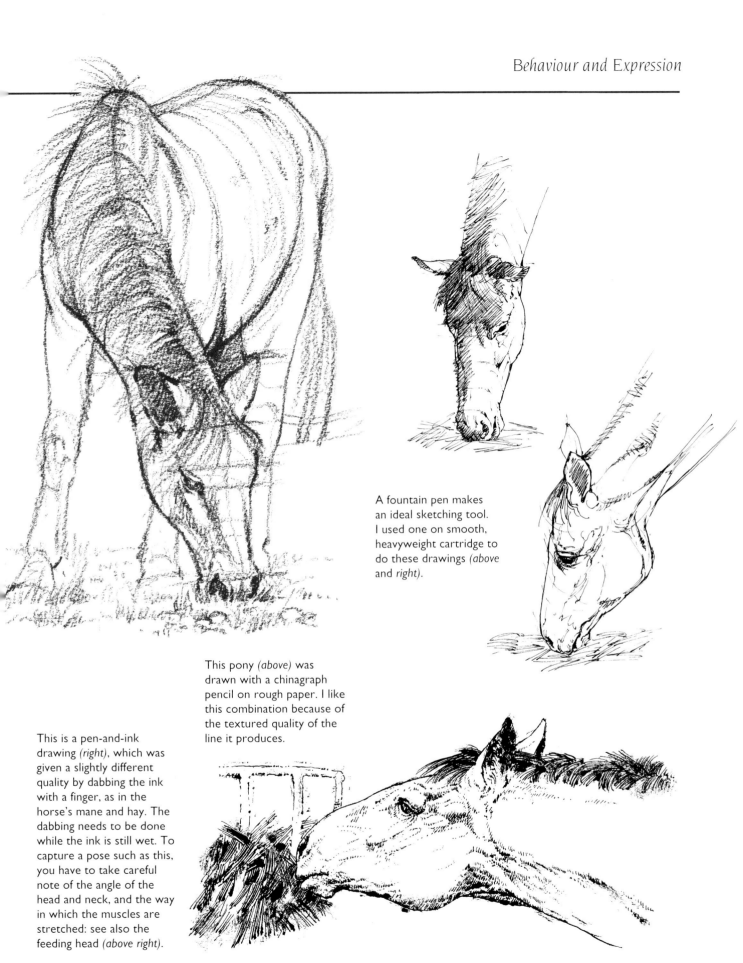

A fountain pen makes
an ideal sketching tool.
I used one on smooth,
heavyweight cartridge to
do these drawings *(above
and right)*.

This pony *(above)* was
drawn with a chinagraph
pencil on rough paper. I like
this combination because of
the textured quality of the
line it produces.

This is a pen-and-ink
drawing *(right)*, which was
given a slightly different
quality by dabbing the ink
with a finger, as in the
horse's mane and hay. The
dabbing needs to be done
while the ink is still wet. To
capture a pose such as this,
you have to take careful
note of the angle of the
head and neck, and the way
in which the muscles are
stretched: see also the
feeding head *(above right)*.

Working from life

When you are first drawing horses 'in action' outdoors, limit yourself to just one medium. If you want to use pencil, take only one medium pencil such as a B, a pencil sharpener and a sketchbook. There is no need to carry an eraser: if you get some lines wrong, just draw them again in the right place. You can erase the lines you are unhappy with later, but it is actually a good idea to leave them in place as they will remind you of your mistakes and how you put them right.

As you become more practised and therefore more confident about working out on location you can add more equipment to your bag. Until then, you will find it more practical not to carry a lot of different tools that you will probably not put into use.

Showing expression

As well as the more active ways of behaving, in their quieter moments horses are also capable of revealing mood and emotion, as careful observation of them will show. Look, for instance, at the two examples here. The mare feeding her foal on the opposite page has a gentle, peaceful expression on her face, while the horse in the drawing below, with its lowered head and eyes, could not look more weary.

I decided to draw this weary character in pastel, which I thought suited the sombre mood. I lightly drew the head using a light pastel pencil, just enough to establish the shape and indicate the position of the features. I then began adding the darker tones, gradually working up to the lighter ones.

Artist's Tip

Don't use too much spray when working with pastels as this will deaden the colours. Apply just a light spray – if you need more you can spray a second and even third time when the previous layer has dried.

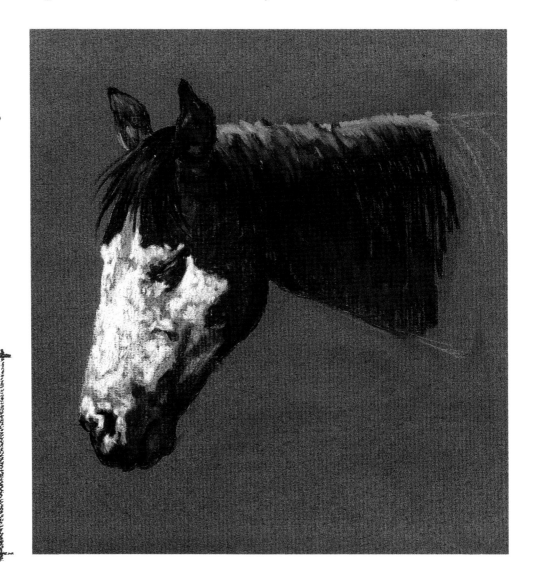

A tender scene, not often witnessed but one that would be a welcome addition to any portfolio. I first drew the basic shape. Then, using the length of the head (line A) as a measuring unit, I quickly checked the accuracy of the proportions. This basic drawing was done with a 2B pencil. The sketch was then overdrawn with a felt-pen, and the pencil lines were erased before applying a wash of clean water. If using this technique, wait until the work is completely dry before sharpening up any lines that have faded under the wash.

Artist's Tip

Use a dry brush to pick out highlights from a freshly applied watercolour wash. If the wash has already dried, use a wet brush first then a dry one.

Movement

It would be impossible to draw a galloping or jumping horse from life: it simply moves too quickly for the eye to follow. Although its head and torso remain relatively static, the position of its legs is constantly changing at a speed too fast for the human eye to capture. As the legs move in different rotation according to gait it is important to get them right, for anyone who is familiar with horses will immediately be able to differentiate between a walk and a canter.

These two sequences *(above* and *above right)* show the series of movements a horse goes through when walking and when galloping. As an experiment, you could try adding further horses to each sequence to complete the series of movements – about two more in each case should be enough.

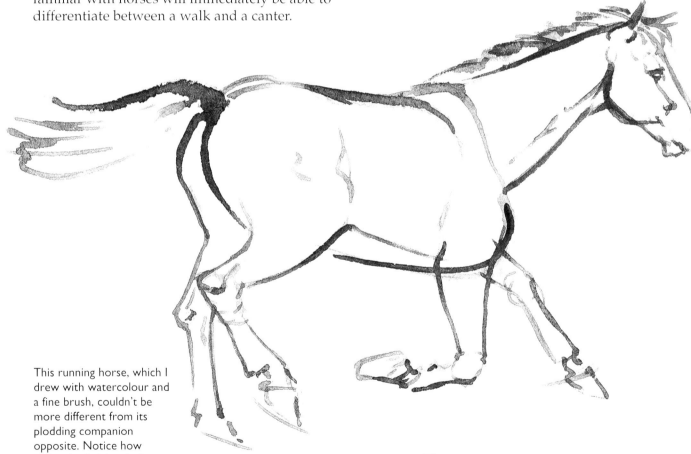

This running horse, which I drew with watercolour and a fine brush, couldn't be more different from its plodding companion opposite. Notice how its head is held up high, and how its tail flicks out behind, as if caught by the wind. As well as being an accurate portrayal of the horse's pose at this moment in time, the angle of its neck and tail helps to create a sense of powerful forward movement. The upper outline of neck, back and tail in fact form one long, continuous, fluid line, like a forward-pointing arrow.

Freeze-frame

Before photography was invented, artists could only guess at how a horse's legs moved at speed – which accounts for the rather strange-looking paintings that you may have seen in art galleries in which the horses appear to be leaping along in mid-air, with all four legs stretched out at the same time.

With the help of photographs of a horse in motion, frame by frame, people were able to see for the first time just how a horse's legs moved at a gallop – and the 'rocking horse' pose with the legs extended and off the ground was proved to be non-existent. If you use photographs for reference, you will be able to see exactly how you should draw the legs.

I drew this plodding horse in charcoal. Notice its lowered neck and head and the downward droop of its tail, all of which create a sense of heaviness, as if the animal just doesn't have the energy to move forward with any speed.

Working from memory

When you are working from life rather than from a photograph, the best approach is to watch the horse for a while before you begin to draw. Once you feel that you have a good visual grasp of its form and movement, draw it swiftly while it is fresh in your memory.

Capturing the essentials

Your purpose when drawing a moving horse is not to produce an accurate, static portrait but rather an impression of a horse in motion. Horses vary in the style of their movement, and generally speaking the more highly bred they are the more graceful and flowing their action. Try to get a sense of this fluidity and rhythm in your rendition of the basic shapes without worrying about details which can be added later.

Speed and size

In order to avoid getting too bogged down in detail, it's best to draw quickly. To help you to get as much movement into your lines as possible, you will also need to draw on a large scale so that your hand is not constrained by tight boundaries. However, don't work on a bigger scale than you feel comfortable with – if you are not at ease your style will reflect this and your drawing will feel cramped and tight no matter how much space there is on the paper.

This energetic conté drawing is a perfect example of how to convey movement with just a few broad strokes. The artist has not concerned herself with irrelevant detail, but has worked loosely, focusing on the main rhythms in the body.

Artist's Tip

Capturing movement can be difficult, so build up a good source of reference material by cutting out any action photographs you come across in newspapers and magazines and keeping them in a folder or box file.

This running horse shows how the basic movement can be captured on paper first, and then detail worked in at a later stage. For this drawing, I used only two pastel pencils for the basic tones, with just a touch of black here and there. The middle tone is created by the colour of the Ingres paper into which I have graded the white and grey pastels.

Starting small

If you find the prospect of drawing the whole horse daunting, ease yourself in by tackling different parts of the body in isolation. Make a study of how the front legs bend as the horse lifts its hooves, then concentrate on the very different angles of the back legs. Draw the angle of the neck in relation to the back and chest and then the head. Building up your confidence in this way will make it easier for you to tackle the whole body because you will have developed a familiarity with its various parts.

The two drawings of jumping horses on this page show a growing sense of confidence. The smaller horse *(above)* is an earlier attempt. I drew the basic outlines first in 2B pencil, then applied a light watercolour wash over the top and emphasized certain of the pencil lines. The horse is seen from the side and at a distance, which made it a simpler and more suitable subject to begin with.

I was closer to the second horse *(left)*, and was looking up at it from a three-quarter viewpoint. This involved a greater use of foreshortening. I used a ballpoint pen for this drawing. Because of its smooth, free-flowing quality, ballpoint can be used on any surface – even a rough one – and is an excellent tool if you want to draw quickly.

Working in this way will sharpen your powers of observation and enable you to gain a fuller understanding of the anatomy of the horse and how it is affected by movement.

You can practically hear the racehorses thundering towards you in this dynamic pencil drawing *(below)*. The tremendous muscular strength and power of these animals is heightened by the dramatic foreshortening of their bodies, which makes them appear wider and bulkier. The bold, diagonal lines made by the pencil further enhance this effect.

Varying the angles

When you are more practised at portraying horses in motion, try drawing them from different angles – perhaps seen from slightly below as a horse jumps a fence, as in the drawing on the opposite page; or even galloping straight towards you, as in the dramatic drawing of racehorses below.

To be able to produce drawings like these involves an understanding and knowledge of foreshortening (see pages 78–9).

Sketching

Sketching teaches you to produce studies of your subject based on accurate observation. It improves your knowledge of form and structure, and is thus an important part of learning to draw.

The purpose of sketching

When sketching, don't get discouraged if your sketches don't turn out perfectly every time. Remember that sketches are *working* drawings only – they are not meant to be beautifully executed pieces of art, worthy of hanging on the wall. Think of each sketch as an exercise, just one of many steps in the whole process.

Your sketchbook is the ideal place to make close-up studies of parts of a horse, as in this head *(above)*. I used a mixture of ballpoint pen and ink wash for this sketch.

Because they are almost impossible to erase, greasy media such as the wax crayon used here *(right)* prevent you trying to 'get it right'. Once a mark is down on paper, it cannot be changed – an excellent discipline when sketching.

I used a ballpoint pen for this sketch. As they are smooth-running, ballpoint pens are an excellent choice of medium for executing quick drawings.

Artist's Tip

Sketching is an integral part of the learning process. Not only do you gather information, you also derive a lot of drawing practice. Don't be put off by the thought of carrying around a large pad and various materials – all you need is a pocket-sized sketchbook and a pencil or ballpoint pen.

Styles of sketching

Sketching can be a matter of making quick, scribbled drawings as you try to portray a horse in action. However, your sketches may also take the form of detailed studies of various parts of the horse which you can refer to for a future drawing or simply use to improve your understanding of anatomy. While sketching you can also take the opportunity to practise using new media and techniques.

Learning to select

To improve your powers of observation and selection, practise this system. First, use your eyes to study the horse, taking note of the basic shapes and angles; then, when it's still fresh in your mind, quickly draw as much as you can remember without looking up again until you have drawn every bit of memorized information.

By drawing from memory in this way, you will realize what information you need in order to make a presentable drawing and – just as important – what to leave out. When you come to repeat the exercise, you will then be more experienced as to what to look for and record.

In no way is this a finished drawing *(left)*, but it contains all the basic information you would need about structure, form and foreshortening to enable you to work up a more detailed piece.

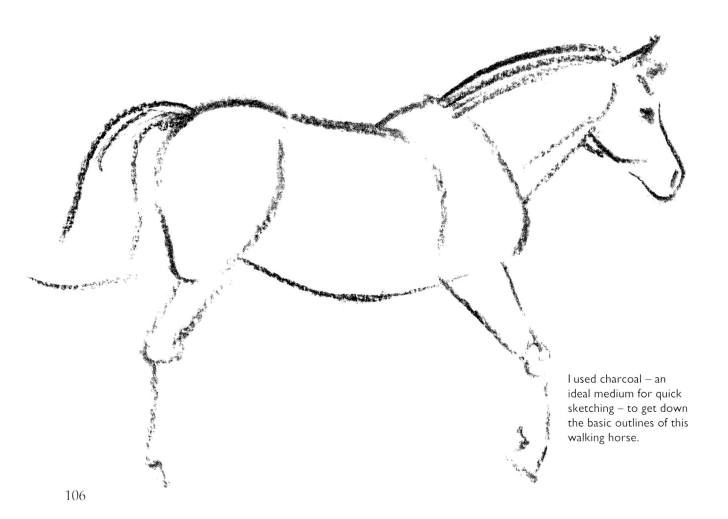

I used charcoal – an ideal medium for quick sketching – to get down the basic outlines of this walking horse.

Good practice

Even if you are not setting out with the purpose of sketching, it is good practice to take a sketchbook and pens or pencils everywhere – you never know when you may come across a scene you feel you want to draw. Get into the habit of sketching often, for this will greatly improve your drawing skills. Try to sketch as many different scenes as possible.

Not only will frequent sketching train your drawing hand, you will also build up a library of reference that you can turn to in the future when you need to be reminded how something looks.

Smudging charcoal is a useful, quick technique for 'blocking in' certain areas, such as this horse's mane and tail.

So that they don't become too smudged, try to fix your charcoal sketches as soon as possible after you have done them.

In Setting

When producing study drawings, it is understandable to focus your attention on the horse alone; you might also do the same if producing the occasional drawing to frame and display on the wall.

Continuing to limit your subject matter in this way would, however, become very boring – to 'complete the picture', you should place your horse in its setting.

One of the most common settings in which you will find horses is with their riders. Horses and riders together may be found at riding schools, at the races or, as here, on the polo field.

Finding your location

You shouldn't have any difficulty in finding horses in different settings. Horseriding is now a very popular sport and there are plenty of riding schools and livery stables all over the country. If you telephone in advance to ask permission to do some sketching or photography the response will probably be a favourable one. Alternatively, you may know someone who is having riding lessons who could introduce you to the owner of the riding school – or, better still, you may even have a friend or acquaintance who actually owns a horse.

If you cannot gain access to any stables, you may know of a field near you where horses frequently graze. Attending agricultural shows or race meetings would provide other sources of material. Finally, while it is always better to work from life, in the last resort you can always turn to your local library.

For this drawing of a horse gazing out above a stable door (opposite), I used pastel pencils on Ingres paper. This paper can be bought in the form of a flip-over pad, in various sizes, making it convenient to carry about.

When doing the drawing, I concentrated on the horse itself, putting in a lot of detail, but kept the surrounding area light so that it wouldn't overpower the head.

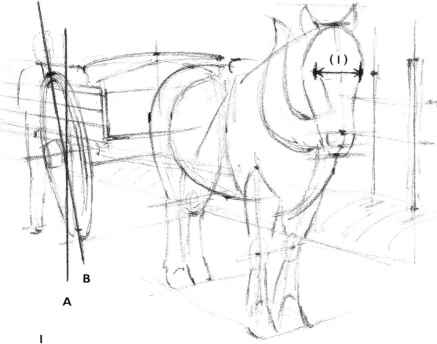

B

A

1

1 To draw this workhorse
and cart, I chose the
distance between the eyes
(1) as my measuring unit,
to check the accuracy of
the proportions before
adding any detail. To check
the angle of the wheel, I
held my pencil vertically
(line A) to find how acute
the angle was (line B).

Safety at work

When you are drawing horses on location, bear
the safety of both you and the horse in mind.
Don't make unexpected movements or loud
noises in close proximity to a horse of whose
temperament you are unsure, and never stand
behind a horse that may kick.

Objects in perspective

Just as the body of a horse is subject to the rules
of perspective (see pages 76–9), so are the
objects that surround it, and this is something
you may have to tackle when drawing a horse
in a particular setting. The cartwheel in the
drawing on the right is a good example.

Seen from this angle, the wheel forms an *ellipse*,
or flattened circle. If you look at the diagram of
the wheel that accompanies the finished
drawing, you will see that the side of the wheel
at C appears wider than it does at D. This
distortion occurs because you are looking at a
perspective view of the wheel – in other words,
you are looking *along* the side of the wheel at C,
but *across* it at D, which creates a foreshortened
effect and makes the outer surface of the wheel
at D appear narrower than it really is.

C

E

D

2

Surrounding objects, such as the fence and the verge of the road, gave me extra reference points for cross-checking the position of key features, and for working out the perspective angles – note the perspective lines drawn across the horse's legs, and along the road and fence.

2 When I was happy that the basic outlines, angles and perspective were correct, I was able to erase unwanted marks and add in detail. Although the horse is, in reality, larger than the driver, the disparity in size appears greater here because of the distorting effects of perspective.

Artist's Tip

When on location you will find it convenient to use a springbound sketchbook. As you open it you can take the front cover right round to the back and the book will remain flat, giving you a stable surface to draw upon.

Cats

Darren Bennett

Choosing the Right Medium

The tool you use, the marks you make, and the surface you draw on all combine in unique and interesting ways. The drawings of a tabby cat's face on these pages are identical in their subject, but not in any other way. Each is created by a different combination of tool and surface. You can almost feel the softness of the fur in some. In others, the emphasis is on the shape of the cat's head. Others highlight the details in the markings of the fur.

Practise using different tools on various surfaces. You'll soon learn to predict the effects you can create, allowing you to choose which to use according to the final appearance you are trying to achieve.

1 Soft pencil on
   cartridge paper
2 Dip pen on
   cartridge paper
3 Charcoal on rough,
   coloured paper
4 Ball-point pen on
   Bristol board
5 Watercolour on
   watercolour paper
6 Coloured pencil on
   cartridge paper
7 Hard pencil on
   cartridge paper
8 Pastel on Ingres
   paper
9 Felt-tip pen on
   layout paper

1

2

3

4

5

6

7

8

9

Measuring in Drawing

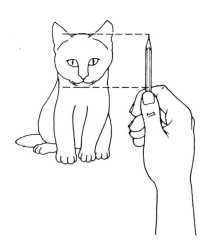

Pencil measuring

Check the accuracy of your drawing by measuring with your pencil. Hold the pencil upright in your outstretched hand. With the point at the top of the object to be measured, move your thumb to the bottom of the object. Keeping your thumb in place, move the pencil to your paper to transfer the measurement.

A useful method when drawing cats is to measure the height of the cat's head and use this as a gauge. See how many of these head heights make up the cat's body. In my drawing below, the kitten's body is one and a half heads high.

One of the easiest mistakes to make, especially when drawing animals, is to misrepresent the relationship among different elements, such as legs, head and body. It helps to understand proportion, which is explained in more detail on pages 118–19. Here are a few tips for quick ways to check that what you see is what's really there.

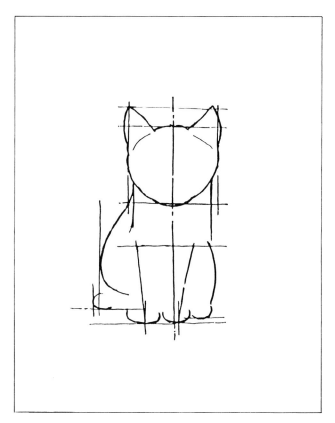

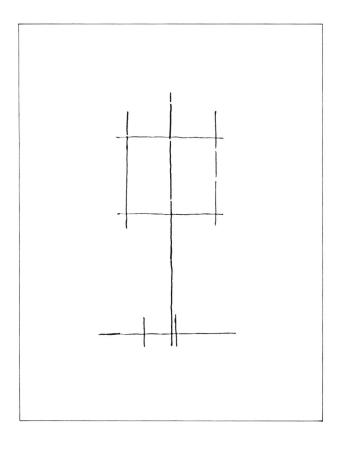

You might be surprised at what you find when using pencil measuring with a central vertical line (*left*) to check your accuracy

I used my pencil to measure the distance from the baseline to the bottom of the chin and the top of the head and ears, drawing horizontal lines at each section (*above*). These horizontals helped me find the right positioning of the kitten's legs in relation to its head

Verticals and horizontals

Another way to check your accuracy is to draw a vertical line down the centre of your page. Use this as the main axis of the cat's body, and relate the positioning of other elements to this vertical. By holding your pencil up vertically, you can see where the cat's shoulders and feet should be placed in relation to this line. The three stages shown on the left illustrate how to build up a drawing from simple verticals and horizontals.

I then used horizontal pencil measuring to help me draw the cat's body in its correct position. I discovered that this kitten's feet are off centre

The final drawing of the kitten (*right*) was drawn using HB and B pencils on cartridge paper

Proportion and Shapes

When drawing cats it helps to understand a few principles of their anatomy.

- A cat's basic body parts are two hind legs, two forelegs, a torso, a neck, and a head. Don't forget the tail, a distinctive feature of most cats.
- A cat's legs are about one-third shorter than the length of its body.
- A cat is usually taller at its hips than at its shoulders.
- A cat's body height is in proportion to its head height.

Getting the proportions right at the basic outline stage is essential.

Seated cat

To draw a seated cat from the front, think of the head in terms of a square and the body as a rectangle in proportion to the head height. The ears are also in proportion to the head.

Use a central vertical line as the main axis, and draw the body in relation to this axis, as described on pages 116–17. Check exactly what you can see from this angle. In the drawing below, for example, three paws are visible.

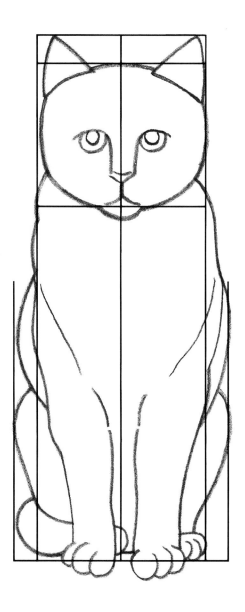

The proportions of a kitten and an adult cat are somewhat different, but the same principles apply to both. When seen from the front in a sitting pose, a full-grown cat's body will be about two and a half times its head height (*left*). A kitten's body in this pose will be less – about one and a half times its head height

The final drawing (*right*) was done in soft pencil on cartridge paper

Standing cat in profile

To draw a standing cat from the side, think of the head again in terms of a square. The cat's torso will be about four times the length of the head, and the tail will be about two times the head length.

Notice that the hind legs are much longer than the forelegs, and that both pairs of legs are shorter than the body length.

Kittens

Cats and kittens have somewhat different proportions. A kitten's head is much larger in relation to its body than a full-grown cat's. Its neck is shorter, and its ears may seem larger in proportion to the rest of its body. Its legs are short and wide, and its feet may seem bigger compared to its body.

A kitten's face has different proportions, as well. Its eyes are big, and its mouth and nose are smaller.

When seen standing in profile, a kitten's body is about two times the length of its head (*left*). In an adult cat in this pose, it is about four times the head length (*below*)

These two drawings were done in B pencil on tracing paper

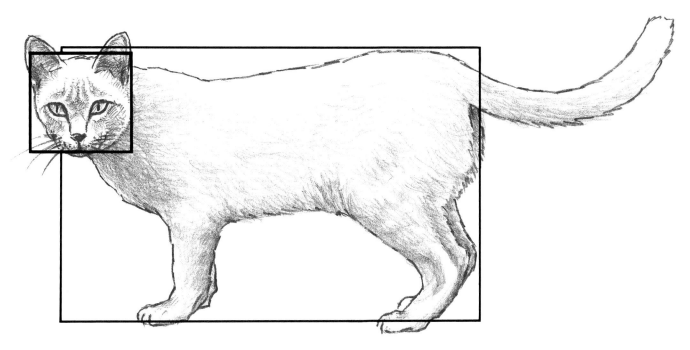

Light and Shade

To convey the sense of a cat's shape, explore the way light bounces and reflects off its surface. This appears on the cat's surface as a range of tones, from white through greys to very black, that create highlights and shadows showing receding and protruding surfaces.

Observe carefully, and understand the source and strength of the light. Strong, direct light creates dark shadows. Light from several directions will produce softer, less dark areas of shadow.

The light shining on the sphere (*above left*) comes from the top left, making the left side bright and the right side darker, as it is in shadow. The same is true of the cat beside it. Light falling from the top left picks out areas of brightness – these are areas that are closest to the source of light. Areas further away, or those where the light doesn't reach, are darker

Like the sphere above, the cat's head (*left*) receives strong light from the top left. Notice that the right eye, which is away from the light, is darker than the left eye. To make your drawing natural, you must carry through the light and shade logic to all elements

Using tone in shapes

Start with just a few tones – such as white and a few shades of grey. As you practise and become more confident, you will learn how to use a wider range of tones to give a sense of colour.

Shadow studies are best done using the block method. Draw your first sketch as though the cat were made of cardboard, with different planes at various angles to the light.

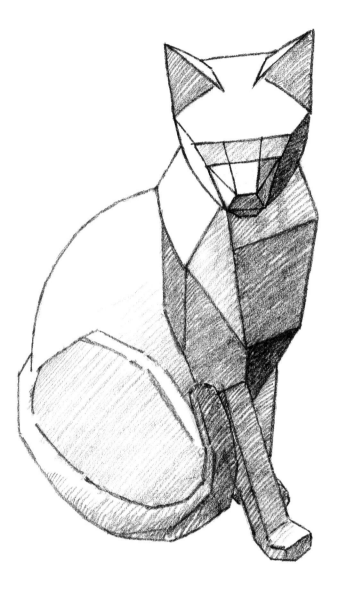

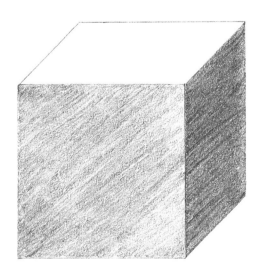

Use a narrow range of tones to shade in the planes that are away from the light, with even darker tones for areas, like the belly, which are also cast in shadow by nearby body parts.

The blocky cat (*above* and *left*) makes it easier to see how areas of the cat's surface are affected by the light or lack of it. Like the cube, which receives strong, direct light from the top left, the top and left side of the cat's body and head are brightest, and the right side and bottom are darkest

Structure and Form

When you draw the full figure of a cat it helps if you think of a number of different aspects of the creature while you work. On these pages you'll find several ways of visualizing a cat's shape.

The silhouette cat
You can probably clearly see the outline shape of the cat, but looking at a silhouette, in which the shape is filled in solid, helps you see proportions more clearly

The skeleton cat
You don't need to study general anatomy, but knowing a little about how the legs are jointed or the feet touch the ground helps you understand the basic frame of the figure

The matchstick cat
Although a very simple way of visualizing a cat's structure, the matchstick figure helps you see clearly the position of the feet and the general posture of the cat

The tin-can cat
Using tubes and other simple geometric shapes can be helpful when trying to create a three-dimensional appearance and when drawing views that are foreshortened or unusual

The main picture of a striped tabby was drawn using HB pencil and finger smudging on thick cartridge paper. It was essential first to get the basic shape right, as the cat's underlying form affects the way the stripes appear in its fur

1

You might feel overwhelmed by the complexity of the cat's form, especially when trying to draw it from a difficult angle. But a cat, like any other living creature or inanimate object, can be thought of as the sum of its individual parts. Think of each part as a familiar shape – a circle, a square, an oval, a triangle. This will make it easier to tackle even the most complex pose.

Practising using shapes
Approach the drawing in stages. Begin with a rough sketch that conveys the basic form and pose in simple shapes (**1**). At each stage add more detail, starting with the eyes and face (**2, 3**) and then completing the details of the body (**4**).

Seeing shapes in poses
The half-sitting, half-standing pose is a common one for cats. For the two sketches opposite, I used overlapping circles for the head and body to get the basic shape, and triangles for ears.

It's usually easier to practise cats' shapes by drawing short-haired cats. Once you feel more confident, try drawing a long-haired cat, like a Persian, using simple shapes. It's harder to see the form beneath all the fur!

2

3

4

Notice all the familiar
geometric shapes in the
walking cat (*left*). Drawing
it in boxy shapes helped
me to focus on the
difficulty of capturing
perspective without
getting caught up in
the details

The cats on these pages
were all drawn in HB
and B pencils on
cartridge paper

Heads and Facial Features

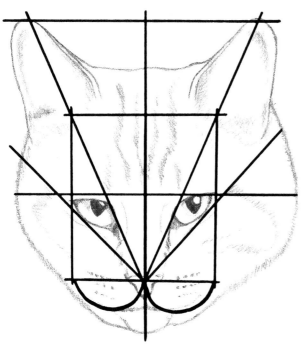

All cats share the basic facial features – eyes, ears, nose, mouth, whiskers – and the same basic relationship among these features. Viewed from the front, this relationship can be shown by breaking down the face into a simple pattern of lines (*left*). Start with a central vertical line which divides the face in half. Then add horizontal lines at regular intervals: top of ears, forehead, above the eyes, at the nose. This is a kind of ladder, with each rung the same distance from the next. Add two more vertical lines at the outside edge of the eyes, then add diagonal lines that intersect this central grid and radiate toward the edge of the face. These relationships are constant. Although there will be some variation among individual cats, use this as the basic model for all frontal cat faces.

Cats of different species have different-shaped heads. Siamese and Burmese cats, for example, have wedge-shaped heads, narrow at the bottom and wider at the top (*right*). Manx and Persians are examples of cats with round heads (*far right*). For both types, begin with a basic circle for the face, and refine the shape as you work

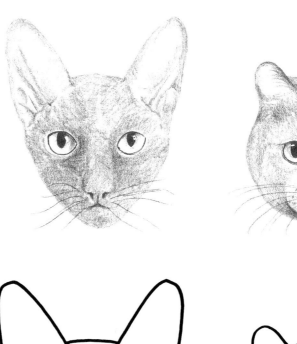

126

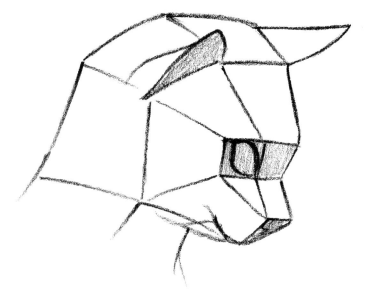

In these blocked heads, the planes of the eyes, the front of the ears, and the end of the nose are parallel. They have been darkened here to emphasize this feature. No matter which way the cat turns its head, these planes will remain parallel

The nose, however, is closer to you than the eyes. You must show it as foreshortened, so that it appears to protrude beyond the other planes to which it is parallel

Perspective

Although the arrangement of facial features is constant, it appears to change when the face is viewed at an angle. When a cat is seen in three-quarter view, for example, its features are seen in perspective, making the eye further away seem smaller than the one closer to you. When viewing a cat in profile, you won't be able to see all of its facial features. But you must always imagine the side you cannot see.

Use the blocking method to practise head forms. Think of the head in terms of planes at angles to one another. Planes that are parallel will remain parallel at any angle. Planes that are closer to you will appear foreshortened.

Draw helping lines in faint pencil wherever you need them as guides to placement – they can always be erased later. And continually check the relationship among the facial features as you work.

Before you draw your cat's face, it is helpful to learn some basic guidelines.

• Use geometric shapes. Seen from the front, a cat's face is either circular or wedge shaped. Its eyes are also circular, but its nose is triangular.

• Use symmetry. A cat's face, like our own, is symmetrical. It is essential to remember this symmetry when you plot the positions of the eyes, ears and cheeks in a drawing that is not a direct frontal view.

Construction
Here is a step-by-step sequence to help you plot the positions of the features on an imaginary cat's face. Do your construction in a soft pencil (3B or 2B) so that these lines are faint and can either be erased carefully or hidden under the detail you add later

1–2 Begin with a simple freehand circle, divided into quarters with lines down and across the centre. Use the cross lines as the frame on which to locate the eyes, nose and mouth
3–4 Remember that the eyes appear about halfway up the face. Draw them first as circles on the line across the centre, then add diagonal lines to show where the brow begins
5 The nose is triangular and is about midway between the horizontal cross line and the chin
6 Place the mouth about midway between the nose and the chin

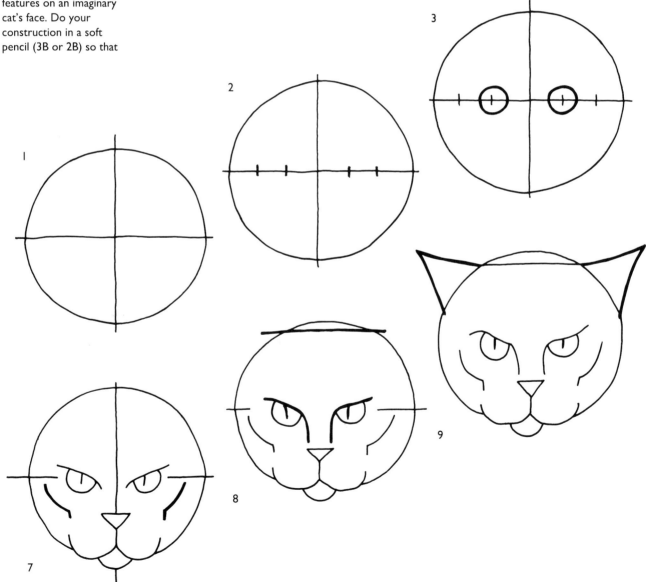

7–10 Now add other lines to define the face, including cheeks and ears. The cheeks add shape, giving the cat's face a ball-like appearance

11–12 Final touches include filling in the pupils and adding whiskers, and going over your final outline with ragged lines to give the appearance of fur. Cats' whiskers grow in regular rows

Cats' eyes
A cat's pupils change their shape dramatically with the amount of light falling on the cat's face (*right*). Unlike our pupils (which change size but not shape), a cat's pupils turn into vertical oval slits when it is looking into a bright light

Side view
A cat's face looks flat from the front but its gentle contours can be seen from a side view (*far right*). The eyes are not sunk deep into the face, but the forehead is rounded and the nose protrudes slightly from the front of the cat's face

Texture and Markings

Building surface texture

Texture is one of the most important aspects of
drawing cats. It is also one of the most enjoyable
tasks, as the great variety of fur textures – long-
haired, short-haired, wire-haired – offers room
for experimentation and exploration.

Carefully observe the surface of the cat you are
drawing. Can you tell what its fur feels like
simply by looking? Notice also that a cat has
several different textures: its collar might be
woolly, its paws less hairy, its cheeks and
forehead soft and downy, its eyes shiny and
smooth. You can portray these different types of
textures using various techniques. Smudge with
your finger to create a soft, blended effect. Use
the smoothness or roughness of the paper to
enhance the texture. A cat's coat can be
smoothed and softened by using finger
smudging, bringing out the underlying texture
of the paper.

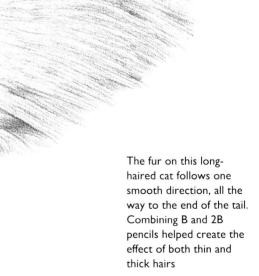

The fur on this long-
haired cat follows one
smooth direction, all the
way to the end of the tail.
Combining B and 2B
pencils helped create the
effect of both thin and
thick hairs

The regular stripes of the American short-haired tabby cover the full extent of its body, from face to tail. Only the paws remain stripeless. It was drawn in 2B pencil on Ingres paper

A Siamese is usually light brown or grey with darker areas around the face, legs and tail. Its short hair makes for smooth, sleek lines. This one (*below*) was drawn in dip pen and ink on watercolour paper

Markings

Fur markings can be fun to draw, since there are many different types: clean or blotchy stripes, spots or patches, even tortoiseshell, a sort of patchwork of black and orange. Observe the markings carefully – often they don't cover the cat's entire body.

You can experiment with fur and markings by drawing a simple cat outline and photocopying it several times. Use these outlines to practise drawing long and short hair and various markings.

Portraying Expressions

Catching cats' expressions is hardest of all.
Every cat not only has distinctive features but
distinctive expressions as well. Compare the two
large pictures on these pages. The cat on the left
has a watchful, almost wary stare. The cat on the
right, though in a similar pose, has a more
curious look, as if eager to play.

One way to practise this task is to make quick
sketches of different expressions as you see
them. Try to capture the emotion by examining
how it changes the features of a cat's face.

The eyes give clues that
are useful when drawing
cats' faces. You can tell
this cat (*below*) is looking
into a bright light because
its pupils appear as narrow
slits. Its expression is a
watchful one

The cats on these pages
were drawn using 2B
and 4B pencils on
different papers.
Notice the difference in
expressions, especially
between the somewhat
wary cat (*below*) and the
hissing cat (*bottom*)

Cats communicate through facial expression; by observation, you will learn how emotions change the appearance of cats' facial features. A happy cat, for instance, perks its ears up; a frightened cat lays its ears flat. Sometimes this will be obvious: a fierce, angry cat, for example, will narrow its eyes and widen its mouth.

Even quick sketches convey much about a cat. Pay attention to the shape of the eyes, ears and mouth – as in these four sketches. These were drawn in B pencil on Kent paper

Sometimes the changes are more subtle. The slight lowering of a cat's head, for example, could indicate that it is unsure if a newcomer is a friend or foe, or, when combined with narrowed eyes, could signal pleasure at being petted.

Cats and kittens show different expressions. A kitten's expression may be one of dumbfounded curiosity, compared to the often wise and composed expressions of older cats. This maturity is also often seen in large, wild cats.

Many adult domestic cats show the same solemn expression as some wild cats, like the jaguar (*above*). Notice the differences and similarities in facial features, especially in the shape of the eyes

The drawing of the wide-eyed Persian (*left*) was done in 2B pencil on tracing paper

135

Sketching

The cat's fur is the most prominent aspect of this drawing, done on watercolour paper in mixed media — 4B pencil, water-soluble pencil and brush, and dip pen and ink

Improving your drawing

Cats are a challenging subject – unless they're sleeping, they usually don't keep still for long. It's likely you won't have a chance to complete a detailed drawing at one time. You'll need patience and lots of practice.

Keeping a **sketchbook** is the best way to practise drawing cats. Don't worry if you have pages of drawings you have had to abandon midway; you can always return to them. Try drawing a cat from different angles to understand how its body works.

At this point it's important not to get caught up in capturing the detail; this can be added later. Try concentrating on just one aspect of the cat: its form, fur, expression, or a gesture.

The Siamese cat stayed in this pose for an unusually long ten minutes, allowing me to produce a quite detailed study of its form using subtle shading obtained with watercolour

I abandoned and returned to this sketch (*top*) several times as the cat moved, but eventually I captured its pose and the half-turn of its head. I used dip pen and ink washes on thick cartridge paper

I used quick strokes in B pencil on cartridge paper to capture the light and shade in this cat's reclining position (*left*)

Be prepared to make many quick sketches to capture the form and energy of the cat. Keep your sketchbook with you and use it to compile a bank of different cat images. One drawing might be a composite of several sketches made at different times.

You can also build up a sketch in different stages. Start with the most basic form, drawing as much of it as you can before the cat changes its pose. You can add to this from memory, defining the cat's pose and then adding details such as facial features.

You can also create a drawing of a group of cats using different sketches from your sketchbook. Overlap them in a way that seems natural so that it appears you drew them all at once.

In this sequence (*above* and *right*), I first drew a quick, rough outline of the cat in my sketchbook while it was in this pose. Using soft pencil on thick cartridge paper, I added detail from memory. I then completed the drawing using dip pen and ink, smudging some areas with my fingertip

These drawings from my sketchbook show the different ways you can use individual sketches

The two poses of the same cat (*top*) were drawn in soft pencil. They were both only half finished before the cat moved on, but I can use them for reference purposes or complete the detail at a later stage

The group of Siamese cats (*right*) is actually the same cat. I used pencil sketches of the cat in three different poses and arranged them to form a new, natural composition, drawn in charcoal

Domestic Cats

Most domestic cats today are either longhairs or shorthairs. Within these two groups, however, are many different breeds, and within each breed are several varieties.

Although all share the same basic body features and some characteristics – such as curiosity and independence – they also display a great range of differences in appearance and behaviour.

The areas of colour on a Siamese get darker as the cat ages, and its elegance is enhanced. This somewhat stylized drawing of a Siamese (*below*) was done in fineline felt-tip marker on layout paper

Persians, for example, are heavy-set and are gentle, adaptable cats. North American shorthairs are hardy and calm. Abyssinians have an unusual, lively look and lithe frames.

This striped tabby kitten was hard to capture on paper – most kittens are excitable and their movements are skittish. For this drawing (*right*) I used H pencil on tracing paper

The easily distinguished Manx cat (*above*) is not only tailless, but its hind section is higher than its front. This gives the Manx its great leaping ability and its peculiar appearance, enhanced in this drawing by the cat's arched back. This was drawn using 2B pencil on watercolour paper

Observe as many types and breeds of cats as possible. You'll soon begin to spot differences among them that will make your drawings more natural and true to life.

Wild Cats

Wild cats cover an even wider range than domestic cats. They are usually divided into large cats – such as the lion, leopard, tiger and jaguar – and small cats, with the cheetah in its own group. Some, like the lion, have strong, heavy frames. Others are quite small – the ocelot, for example, is only about twice the size of the typical domestic cat. (The cats on these pages, all on cartridge paper in different media, are not drawn to scale.)

A Pallas's cat (*above*)
in B pencil

A caracal, with distinctive
tufted ears, in coloured
pencil (*right*)

The slender African serval
in 2B pencil

A red lynx (*left*) in
HB pencil

A snow leopard with its
heavy tail (*above*) in ballpoint pen

The fastest animal, a
cheetah (*left*), in fineline
felt-tip marker

A tiger, one of the largest
cats, in coloured
pencil (*below*)

Like domestic cats, wild cats display a variety of
interesting patterns: spots, patches, stripes and
even, as on the jaguar, large rosettes. Often the
pattern doesn't cover the entire animal. Also, no
two animals have identical markings.

Look through nature magazines to find pictures
of wild animals, or – for a bigger challenge – go
to the zoo and draw them from life!

Cat Behaviour

Cats sleeping

Cats sleep for up to two-thirds of their lives, so at some point you're likely to want to draw a sleeping cat. This is the ideal occasion for practising the cat's form, as it is sure to be still for at least a short time. Take advantage of the moment!

You won't always have time for detailed drawings, however. Cats usually take several brief 'catnaps' during the day, so it is still important to do quick sketches to try to capture the pose before the cat moves.

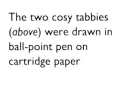

The two cosy tabbies (*above*) were drawn in ball-point pen on cartridge paper

These mounds of fur are really a sleeping tortoiseshell cat (*above*) and a tabby kitten and its solid-coloured mother (*left*), all drawn on cartridge paper in HB pencil

A red tabby shorthair
caught at the moment just
before falling into a deep
sleep, drawn in B pencil
(*above*), and fast asleep,
drawn in ball-point
pen (*below*)

One difficulty with drawing sleeping cats is that
they are often tightly curled up so they resemble
shapeless furry bundles. Remember what you
know about the cat's underlying form – its basic
anatomy – even if you cannot see it clearly in
your subject.

The pattern on this silver
tabby (*right*) becomes
even more interesting
when the cat is wrapped
tightly into a ball. It was
drawn on cartridge paper
in 4B pencil

Stationary cats

It may be difficult to move from drawing still, sleeping cats to capturing active cats in motion. The two tasks are very different. One way to ease this transition is to experiment with stationary cat activities, such as washing and eating. These activities are slower than action and so are less demanding, but the slight motion that is involved adds a sense of movement to the lines of your drawing.

Grooming

Each cat has its own grooming routine. Most, however, wash themselves by licking their paws and rubbing them over their face and ears. If you watch carefully over a period of time, you'll learn to predict the cat's next grooming move. This will also help if you need to refine your drawing later from memory.

Eating

Eating involves little movement, and it is a pose cats stay in for several minutes, making it useful for practice.

A cat's paws and head are the most important body parts in the grooming ritual. You can almost feel the movement in these sketches: washing the forehead (*top left*), in B pencil on cartridge paper; licking the paw clean (*left*), in B pencil on cartridge paper; and grooming the whiskers and face fur (*above*), in 2B pencil on cartridge paper

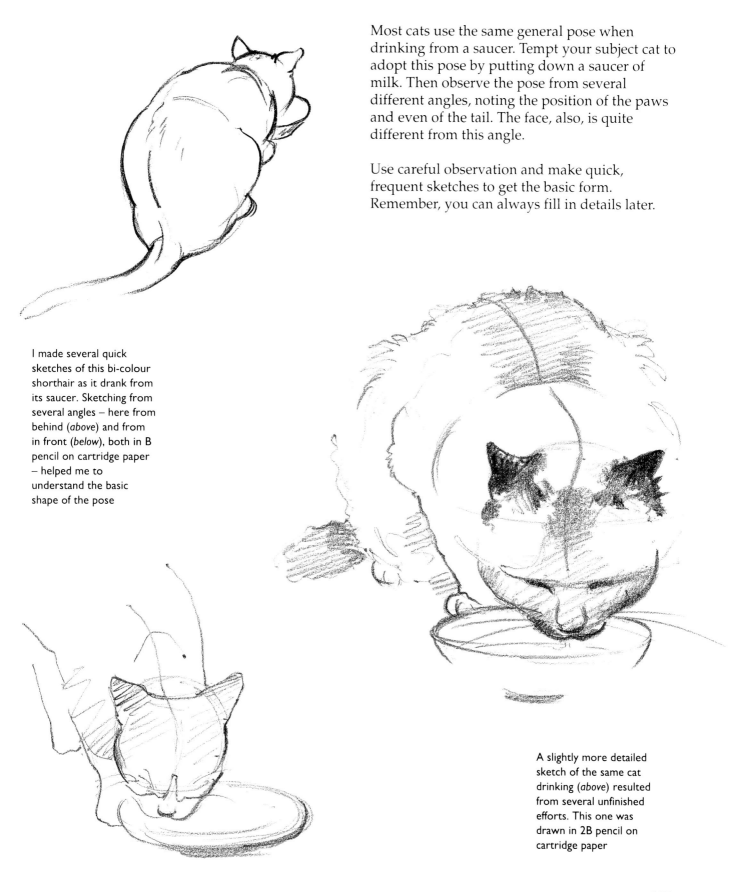

Most cats use the same general pose when drinking from a saucer. Tempt your subject cat to adopt this pose by putting down a saucer of milk. Then observe the pose from several different angles, noting the position of the paws and even of the tail. The face, also, is quite different from this angle.

Use careful observation and make quick, frequent sketches to get the basic form. Remember, you can always fill in details later.

I made several quick sketches of this bi-colour shorthair as it drank from its saucer. Sketching from several angles – here from behind (*above*) and from in front (*below*), both in B pencil on cartridge paper – helped me to understand the basic shape of the pose

A slightly more detailed sketch of the same cat drinking (*above*) resulted from several unfinished efforts. This one was drawn in 2B pencil on cartridge paper

Cats in action

Watching cats move is a pleasure. Their grace, even in sudden moves, can be difficult to capture on paper, however. It helps to understand something about how a cat moves. Observe the way it walks: which feet move and in what order. Knowing the basics of cat movement will make your action drawings more real and believable.

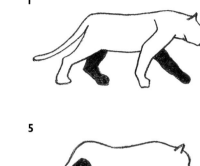

Catwalk basics

Cats move in a great variety of ways: they prowl, leap, run and walk. Here are a few basics to keep in mind.

● When walking, a cat moves in the following sequence: right rear leg, right front leg, left rear leg, left front leg, and so on.

The sequence here (*above* and *right*) shows a nearly grown kitten first playing with its prey, then pouncing. Drawing a sequence gives a sense of fluidity. I drew this in 2B pencil on cartridge paper

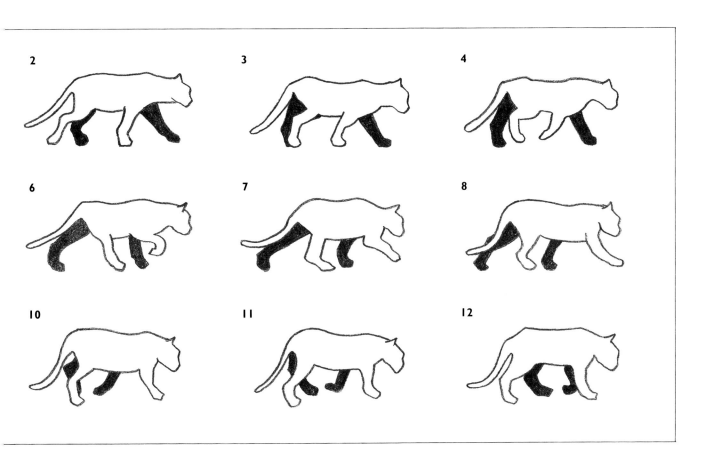

The twelve steps of a
cat's walk (*above*). I
shaded in the legs on the
opposite side of the cat to
make it more clear which
legs move when

• A walking or running cat will always have two feet on the ground, and even when pouncing, cats often keep their rear paws firmly on the ground.
• A cat's tracks appear almost as a straight line because a cat carefully places one foot in front of the other.

Sequencing

One way to capture action is to draw a sequence. Each new stage of your sequence will show a slightly different pose as the cat moves. To do this, make rapid sketches, one after the other, moving from one unfinished sketch to another. You won't have time to finish a drawing, complete with detail, for each stage. Instead, focus on capturing the form and essence of the movement. Add details of texture and shading later.

Dogs

David Brown

Choosing the Right Medium

1

2

Of all the drawing tools available to the artist, the humble pencil is probably the most common and the most favoured. The popularity of the pencil is understandable. First of all, it is a very convenient tool, being light, small, and therefore easy to transport. Compared with charcoal, pastel, or pen and ink, it is much less messy to use – another reason that makes it more portable, for there are no risks of spills or smudges in transit. And finally, the pencil is cheap to buy and can easily be obtained in stationery and art shops.

Although the pencil has many advantages, it would be a great pity if you limited yourself to this medium alone and did not experiment with others. Only by experimenting with other media will you discover the kind of effect each produces. A time will come when you'll want to create a particular effect in your drawing and you will need to know which medium to choose.

However, it isn't your drawing tool alone that will produce a specific 'look'. The marks you put down on your drawing surface will be affected by the nature of that surface – whether it is rough or smooth, how absorbent it is, and so on. Experiment with different media on different surfaces to see how various combinations work.

In the pictures on these two pages, I have produced six drawings of the same dog. I am indebted to Chris and Shirley, two friends of mine, for allowing me to draw their dog Ria to illustrate how much her appearance changes with each change of medium and surface.

1 Dip pen and ink on smooth cartridge
2 Felt pen on medium cartridge
3 Watercolour on watercolour paper
4 Pastel pencil on grey Ingres paper
5 2B pencil on CS2 'not' paper
6 Charcoal pencil on watercolour paper

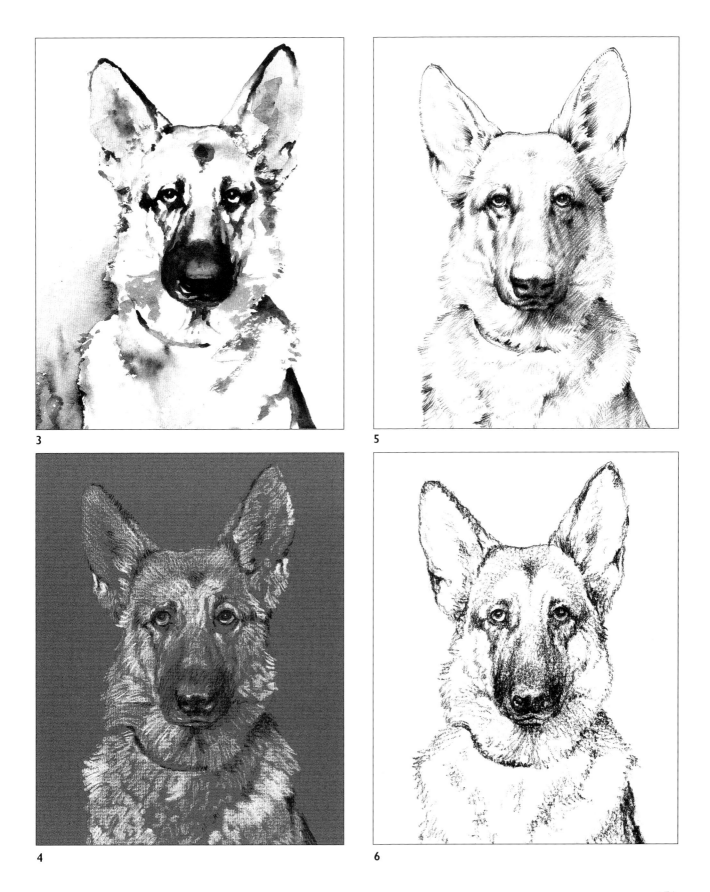

3

5

4

6

Proportion and Measuring

In order to produce good drawings of animals, whether of the farmyard variety or any other type, you need to master the basic elements of proportion – the sizes of the different parts in relation to each other.

For many people, this aspect of drawing presents one of the biggest problems. However, if you want your work to bear a convincing resemblance to the real thing, it is vital to get the proportions right. If the underlying structure is wrong, you will not be able to disguise the fact with shading or colour.

The pencil method

A simple but effective method of achieving this level of accuracy is illustrated below. Choose a portion of your subject – say, the head of the dog – and use this as your *measuring unit*. Hold your pencil at arm's length and line up the top of it with the top of the dog's head. Now place your thumb on the pencil to line it up with the bottom of the head. You now have a unit which you can use to measure how many head lengths make up the length of the body; by holding the pencil horizontally, you can also tell how many make up the width.

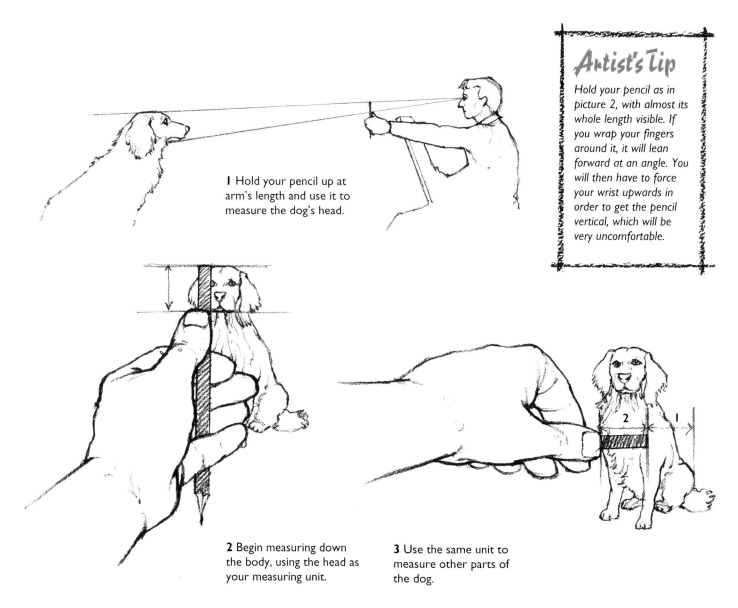

Artist's Tip

Hold your pencil as in picture 2, with almost its whole length visible. If you wrap your fingers around it, it will lean forward at an angle. You will then have to force your wrist upwards in order to get the pencil vertical, which will be very uncomfortable.

1 Hold your pencil up at arm's length and use it to measure the dog's head.

2 Begin measuring down the body, using the head as your measuring unit.

3 Use the same unit to measure other parts of the dog.

When measuring in this way, remember always to keep your arm straight, your pencil vertical, and your thumb on the same spot on the pencil.

The eye test
To find out how well you are able to judge proportions without measuring them, try this simple test. First choose your subject. It could be a live dog or you could use a photograph, but it should be a good picture, and the larger it is, the better. For this purpose, a photograph may, in fact, be better because the subject won't move while you are doing your test, and you'll more easily be able to check the accuracy of your drawing afterwards.

Now do a drawing of the dog, keeping it very simple. For this test, don't bother putting down any of the detail: if you wish, you need do no more than make a series of marks on the paper to indicate the proportions – the size of the head, and how long or wide you think the body, the legs and other parts of the dog should be in comparison to the head.

Checking for accuracy
Now compare your drawing with the dog in the photograph, or your live subject. Use the 'pencil method' already described – of course, if you have worked from a photograph, you don't have to do this at arm's length – and make a note of the results.

Now check your drawing in the same way. How well do the proportions in your drawing match those in the photograph, or those of the live dog?

In this drawing, I used the measuring method to check the size of the various parts of the body against each other. I then marked out these measurements to form the basis of my drawing. When the drawing looks right, the measuring marks can be erased.

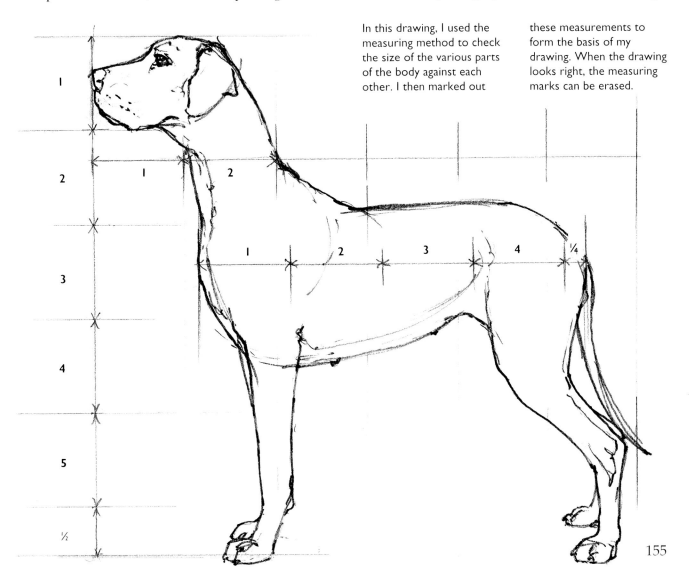

155

1 To draw this Airedale Terrier, I first roughly sketched a simplified shape. Then I took the distance from the outer edge of the nose to the top of the head and used this as my measuring unit (A).

Training your eye

To start with, it is best to use the pencil method of measuring for your basic drawing – this will form the foundation of the finished work so it is important to get the proportions and angles right. As you progress, however, you will become more practised at assessing proportions and will be able to judge them by eye, only needing to use the pencil method to check your drawing if it looks wrong.

As you work, train your eye by continually comparing the sizes of the various different parts. For example, do the front legs appear longer than the back legs? How does the length of the neck compare with that of the legs? How does the the head compare with the body? How do the widths compare?

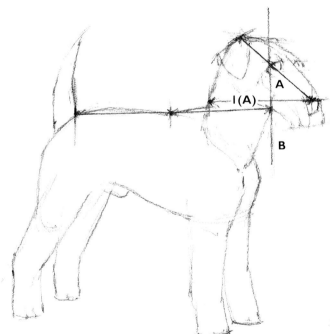

2 Holding the measure horizontally, I discovered that the distance from the nose to the back of the neck – 1(A) – was the same as line A. Holding the pencil vertically, I saw that the point at which the head met the neck lined up with the back of the eye (B). Holding the pencil vertically in this position also showed me the angle at which the dog held its neck.

3 When I had compared and corrected all the proportions and marked in the position of the key details, I worked up the finished drawing using a chinagraph pencil.

Using a plumbline

A plumbline is a simple device used for checking angles, and you can easily make one yourself by tying a small weight on the end of a piece of string or cotton. To work the plumbline, all you have to do is hold the end of the string and allow the weight to hang free to give you a true vertical line.

Although this method is more accurate than using a pencil, it does have one disadvantage – as you move the plumbline across the body from one part to another, you will need to use both hands to steady the weight and prevent it swinging from side to side.

A plumbline provides a simple tool that will enable you to check vertical lines and angles.

Artist's Tip

Draw your 'construction lines' lightly so that they can be covered with shading or else erased when your outline drawing is complete.

Structure and Form

If you take the trouble to learn a little about the underlying anatomy of a dog's body, it will give you a better understanding of the surface form – and you'll produce more convincing drawings.

Where to begin

The best way to start learning about canine anatomy is by finding suitable references to study. Your local library may stock books on dog health and care, and these will almost certainly contain helpful diagrams. Failing that, you should be able to find books on dog anatomy at your nearest natural history museum.

Bones and muscles

Unless you intend to specialize professionally, you don't need to make a serious study. However, it would be most useful to develop a general knowledge of the way in which the muscles lie and interconnect, as well as the structure of the bones, especially those closest to the surface which affect its shape most.

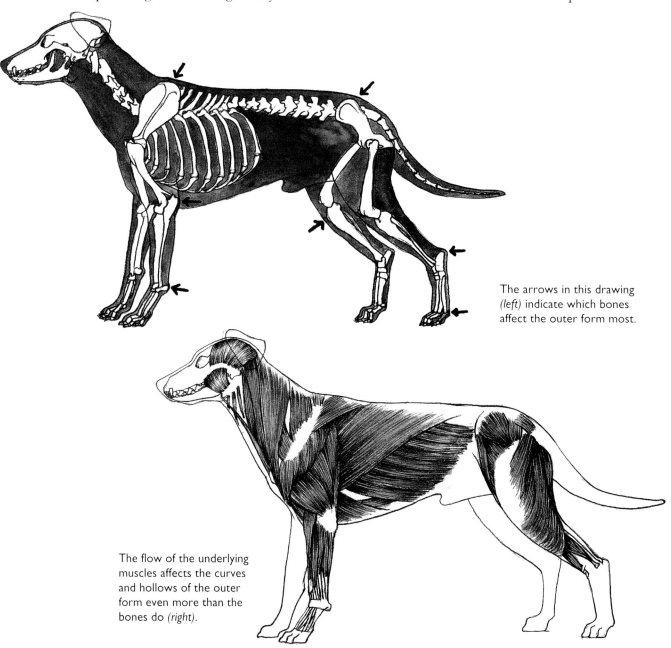

The arrows in this drawing *(left)* indicate which bones affect the outer form most.

The flow of the underlying muscles affects the curves and hollows of the outer form even more than the bones do *(right)*.

Linear perspective makes objects appear progressively smaller as they recede. To understand how it works, imagine that there are two lines on either side of the object you are drawing which increasingly slant inwards towards each other as the object recedes – if the lines continued they would eventually join together at a point known as the vanishing point. In these two drawings, compare lines A and I(A) and B and I(B) to see how this 'slanting' effect alters the shape of the dog's body.

Perspective

The optical illusion known as perspective allows artists to draw objects that look three-dimensional on a flat, two-dimensional surface. If you want your drawings of dogs to look convincing, you'll need to learn how this artist's 'trick of the trade' works.

Perspective may be divided into three types – linear, tonal or aerial, and foreshortening – all of which may be used to convey a sense of solidity, depth and distance.

Linear perspective is probably the most widely known of these three types of visual illusion. According to this, objects appear smaller the further they are from the person viewing them. So a dog standing close to the viewer will look larger than a dog further away, even though, in reality, they may both be exactly the same size.

Tonal perspective affects the depth of tone and definition of objects, and is caused by an atmospheric trick which progressively subdues colours and the differences between light and shade according to how far objects are from the viewer. On a dog's body, of course, one end is hardly far away enough from the other to make a difference – but for artistic effect, you could 'cheat' and exaggerate the gradual change in tone and detail to emphasize the sense of three-dimensional depth. This is what is known as 'artist's licence'!

This drawing illustrates the effect of tonal perspective *(left)*. The lighter tones used for the dog on the right push it into the background, while the darker tones of the dog on the left 'bring it forward'. The differences in tone have been deliberately exaggerated to produce this effect. Tonal perspective can be used to convey depth when the subjects are too close together to use linear perspective.

> ## Artist's Tip
>
> *When producing a study drawing, keep to very simple shapes. You will then find it easier to understand the structure and to check angles and proportions.*

In this sketch *(right)*, compare the amount of detail and weight of line used in the dog's head with that in the body.

Foreshortening is a form of extreme linear perspective. As the name implies, it describes the way perspective distorts the different parts of the same object, making certain parts appear to 'shorten' and become condensed as they recede. Sometimes these parts shrink so much that they almost disappear. When dealing with foreshortening, therefore, it is all the more important to use the measuring method described on pages 154–5, so that you draw what you *see*, not what you *know* to be there.

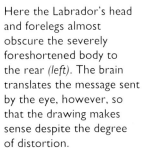

The foreshortening in this drawing of a Pointer *(above)* is so severe that the body and hind legs virtually disappear.

Here the Labrador's head and forelegs almost obscure the severely foreshortened body to the rear *(left)*. The brain translates the message sent by the eye, however, so that the drawing makes sense despite the degree of distortion.

Looking at Features

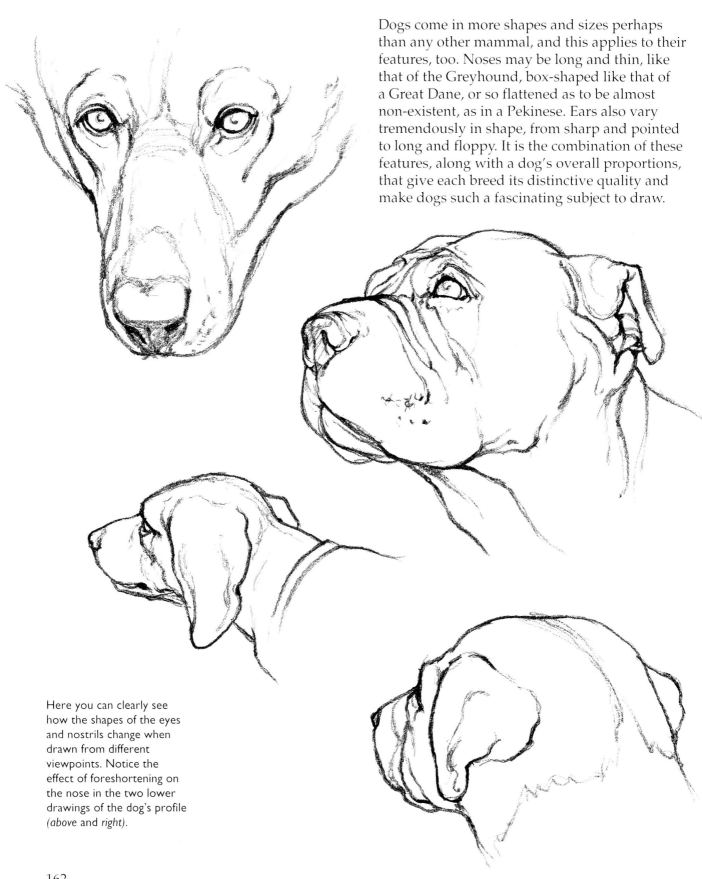

Dogs come in more shapes and sizes perhaps than any other mammal, and this applies to their features, too. Noses may be long and thin, like that of the Greyhound, box-shaped like that of a Great Dane, or so flattened as to be almost non-existent, as in a Pekinese. Ears also vary tremendously in shape, from sharp and pointed to long and floppy. It is the combination of these features, along with a dog's overall proportions, that give each breed its distinctive quality and make dogs such a fascinating subject to draw.

Here you can clearly see how the shapes of the eyes and nostrils change when drawn from different viewpoints. Notice the effect of foreshortening on the nose in the two lower drawings of the dog's profile (*above* and *right*).

Changing viewpoints

When you change your viewpoint, you will be seeing a dog's features from a different angle so they will be a different shape. To get a feeling for each feature 'in the round', study the head from various positions. The three main viewpoints are full view (head on), full profile, and the three-quarter view which is a combination of both. Do sketches from these three viewpoints and observe how the shape of the features gradually shifts, flattening or elongating as the head turns.

The front view of this Pomeranian *(left)* gives little clue to the shape of its nose in profile.

Features

No single feature exists independently of the others: they all slot together to make up the whole like parts of a complex, three-dimensional jigsaw puzzle.

When you do your drawing, observe how the different features interrelate, and how one form flows into or moulds itself around the next. How do all these forms fit together to make up the total structure of the head? Where, for example, are the eyes positioned in relation to the nose? How do the ears 'sit'?

In profile, the Pomeranian's sharply pointed snout and curved forehead are revealed *(below)*.

Artist's Tip

Imagine that you could trace a finger around a dog's head and 'feel' the shapes: where they are broad and flat, where they are rounded, or hollow. Now translate these contours into actual 'construction' lines on your drawing.

Ears

Ears are quite complex in structure – even those that appear simple at first can prove difficult to draw when studied in detail. Placing the ears correctly on the head can also be a little tricky.

To make ears easier to draw, use your pencil as a tool to check how the various features line up with one another. Check the relative angles, too, and if you wish include these guidelines in your drawing (you can always erase them later).

In the drawings below, you can see how a line drawn across the head shows how the base of the ear, the eye and the tip of the nose align with each other. In the other drawings, notice how the guidelines and angles have been used to help establish the positions of the various features. Look, too, at how the ears seem to 'grow' out of the head.

The angle and shape of the ears can differ dramatically from one breed to another. Here I have drawn a few of the more obvious differences. Dogs can also move their ears, momentarily changing shape. For example, when showing fear or submission they will flatten their ears. They will also use one ear only to locate a sound which interests them, or prick up both ears in order to catch a sound.

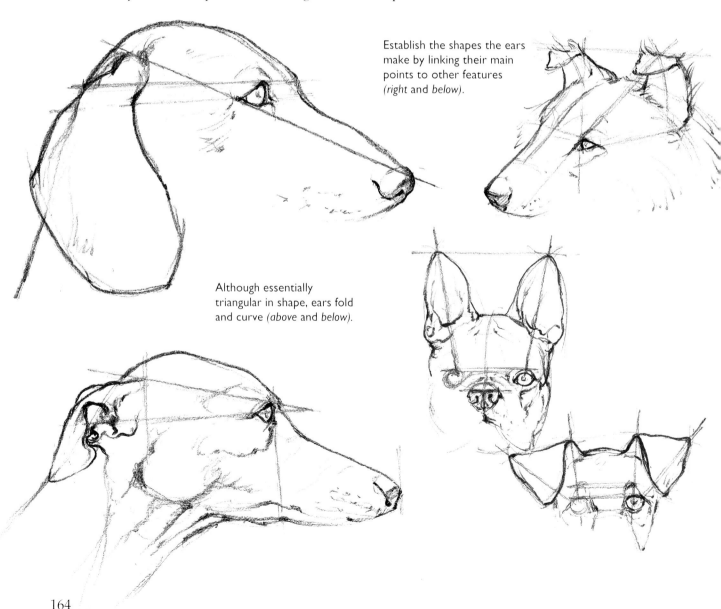

Establish the shapes the ears make by linking their main points to other features (*right* and *below*).

Although essentially triangular in shape, ears fold and curve (*above* and *below*).

Nostrils

Nostrils can be difficult to draw out of context, so I advise you to include as much of the surrounding area as possible when doing your study drawings, as this will make them easier to 'read' visually. Carefully study the structure of the nostril and what happens to it when viewed from different positions.

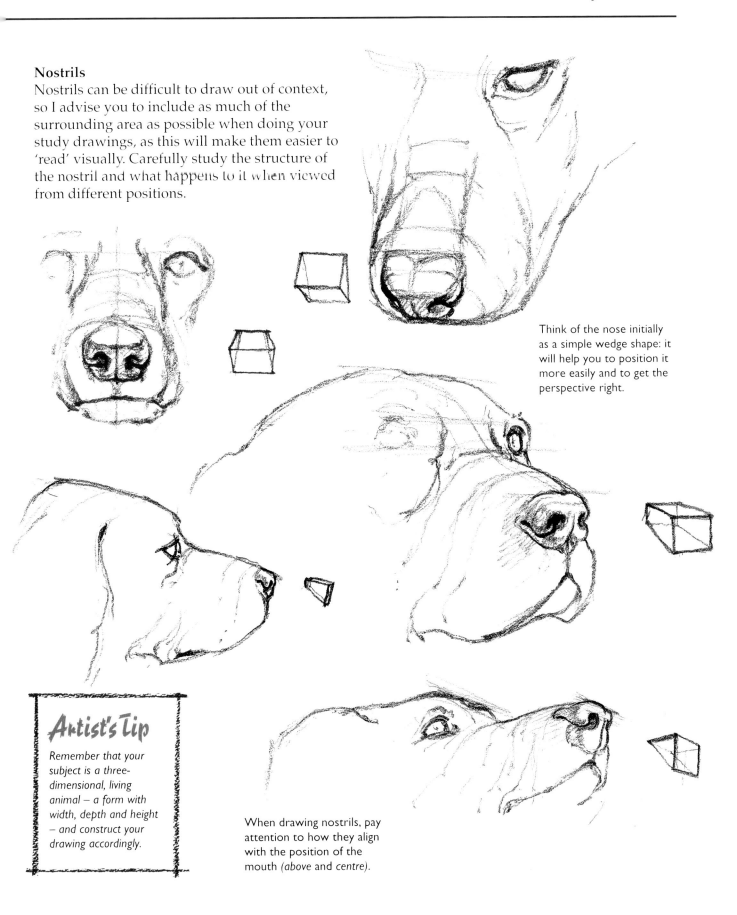

Think of the nose initially as a simple wedge shape: it will help you to position it more easily and to get the perspective right.

Artist's Tip

Remember that your subject is a three-dimensional, living animal – a form with width, depth and height – and construct your drawing accordingly.

When drawing nostrils, pay attention to how they align with the position of the mouth *(above* and *centre).*

Different Breeds

There are many breeds of dog, each of them with its own distinct character formed by a combination of size, shape, coat and markings. It would be impossible to show all the different breeds in this book, and on occasion I have had to show a breed more than once in order to illustrate a certain point – as in *Choosing the Right Medium* – but, within the limitations of the space available, I have tried to show as many breeds as possible.

One way to familiarize yourself with the characteristics of the various breeds is to find visual references for them, and make drawings of these. As you build up your reference drawings, study what it is that makes one breed different from another. For instance, in what details does a Corgi differ from a Basset Hound? Look also at the way in which age affects a dog's appearance: how does a puppy differ from a fully grown adult of the same breed?

This Dachshund *(right)* was drawn on a semi-rough cartridge paper, using a B grade pencil. The most distinctive characteristic of this breed is the extreme shortness of its legs in relation to the head and body, which are of comparatively normal proportions.

This Fox Terrier *(left)*, drawn in black and white conté on grey Ingres paper, has the muscular build of a dog made for running. Its head is fairly large in proportion to its body, and its back legs are widely splayed, with the strong backward thrust needed to propel it forwards.

Key differences

Apart from very obvious characteristics such as
the length of a dog's coat, leg length can be one
of the most striking differences between
different breeds. Other key features to look at
include the shape of the head – is the nose long
and pointed or square-shaped? The shape and
set of the ears is usually also very distinctive;
are the ears pointed and held upright, or long,
rounded, and floppy?

Compare this Weimaraner,
which I drew with conté
crayon on heavyweight
cartridge, with the
Dachshund opposite. Head
and ears are not dissimilar,
and the body of the
Weimaraner does narrow
considerably towards the
rear – the real difference,
though, lies in the relative
leg lengths.

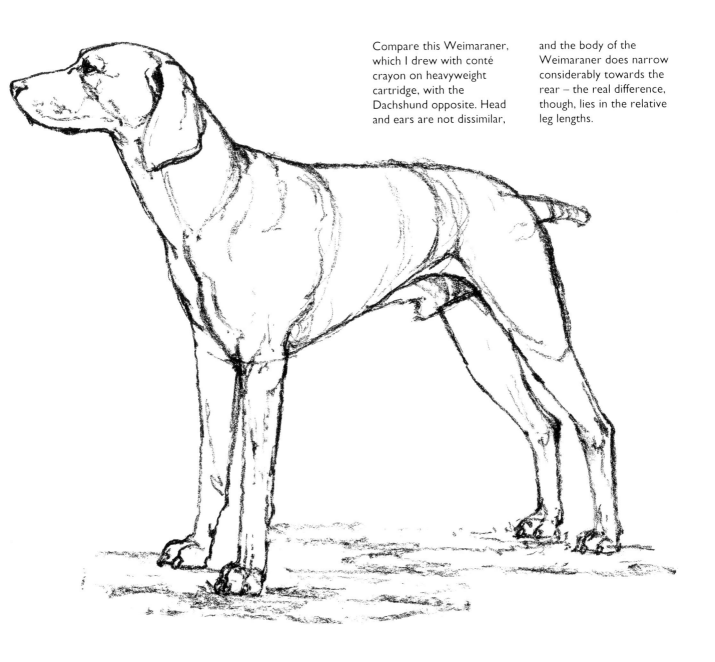

Short-haired dogs

In short-haired breeds, the anatomical structure of the animal is fully visible and so has a powerful visual impact. For this reason, these are good breeds to draw to begin with, when you are trying to familiarize yourself with canine anatomy. Short-haired breeds include the more muscular types, many of whom are sometimes used as guard dogs, such as the Dobermann Pinscher, Mastiff, Bull Terrier, and Boxer. The Boxer, shown below, is a German cross-breed of the Bullenbeiszer and Bulldog.

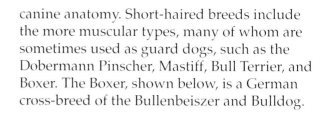

1 I began this drawing of a Boxer by doing a quick sketch, checking the proportions as I progressed.

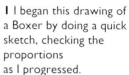

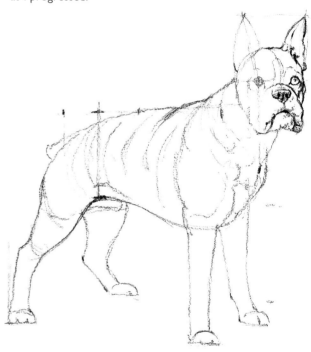

2 I then did a more detailed drawing with a charcoal pencil over the top of the basic sketch, which I then fixed using a can of colourless fixative.

3 Finally I put on a wash to indicate the coloured patches on the dog's coat.

Long-haired dogs

The anatomical structure of a long-haired dog is partly obscured by its coat, which then becomes one of its most striking features. Apart from those breeds that immediately spring to mind, such as the Afghan Hound, there are long-haired types in many other breeds. For example, the Dachshund already portrayed on page 166 appears not only as the well-known short-haired dog, but also in long-haired and wire-haired versions. In the Labrador group, in addition to the smooth-coated variety, there are the longer-haired versions such as Curly-coated, Flat-coated and Golden Retriever.

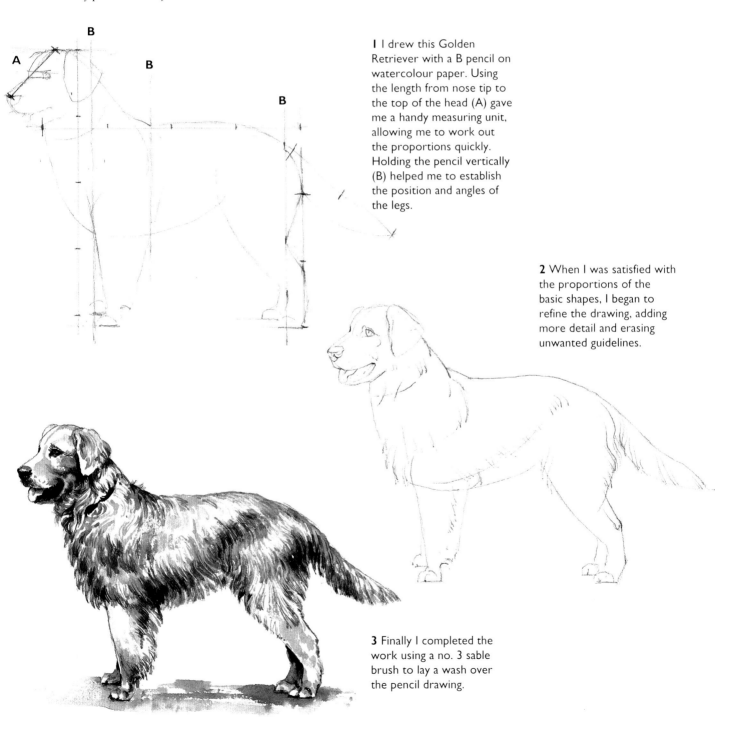

1 I drew this Golden Retriever with a B pencil on watercolour paper. Using the length from nose tip to the top of the head (A) gave me a handy measuring unit, allowing me to work out the proportions quickly. Holding the pencil vertically (B) helped me to establish the position and angles of the legs.

2 When I was satisfied with the proportions of the basic shapes, I began to refine the drawing, adding more detail and erasing unwanted guidelines.

3 Finally I completed the work using a no. 3 sable brush to lay a wash over the pencil drawing.

Texture and Markings

Conveying the various textures and markings on different breeds of dog not only takes skill, but also depends on choosing the medium – or media – that is most likely to produce the effect you want. The more you practise using different media, the better your skill in handling them, and the more appropriate your choice of medium will be.

Variety of texture
Throughout the many breeds you will come across three basic textures: short hair, which gives the dog a smooth appearance; long, flowing hair; and curly hair. In addition to these textures are the colours and markings of the various breeds.

Reproducing the soft quality of the hair on a dog's coat using only a pencil on a two-dimensional surface can seem a daunting task to the inexperienced. A method I like is to use a soft pencil on a smooth to semi-rough paper. You can produce very subtle lines by holding the pencil lightly, exerting very little pressure when drawing an area of hair affected by light, and increasing the pressure when drawing hair in the shaded areas. Initially I draw individual lines following the direction in which the hair is growing, taking care to place lines extremely close to each other for a velvety effect.

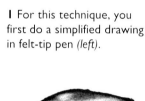

I For this technique, you first do a simplified drawing in felt-tip pen *(left)*.

I These two drawings show one of the ways to achieve a smooth effect with pencil. First do your pencil drawing, adding gentle shading where required *(above)*. Here I used a B pencil on smooth cartridge.

2 Then smudge the shading with your finger or French stick *(right)*. Notice how smudging makes the shading darker. If you find that some areas are too dark or hard-edged, dab them with a putty eraser. Smudging has a tendency

to even out the tones which can sometimes result in a grey drawing that lacks depth. If this happens, accentuate the darker areas to regain the depth.

2 Then dip a brush into clear water to make it damp but not too wet. Run the tip along the inside of the lines only to dissolve the ink slightly and create a shaded effect *(above)*. This technique works best on paper or board with a smooth surface.

1 This is Sam whom I was kindly allowed to draw by his owner Pam. Sam was drawn with a 4B pencil on semi-rough cartridge. I first roughly drew the shape. Using the length from the tip of the nose to the top of the head (A) gave me a measuring unit, allowing me to check the proportions.

2 When I was satisfied with the proportions of the basic shapes, I began to refine the drawing, adding more detail.

3 Finally, I completed the details showing the flow of the hair and adding shadings, as described above, to indicate the three-dimensional shape of the dog.

Artist's Tip

Creating a sense of texture is to do with 'seeing' what something feels like. So, when working out what effect to create, imagine you could touch your subject. Does it feel smooth and velvety? Coarse and rough? Choose your materials accordingly.

Behaviour and Expression

Dogs display a range of both body and facial expressions, from terrifying aggression to sheer joy when greeting their owners. The dog is a hunter and pack animal by nature, which makes it sociable within its own group but prepared to defend its territory against outsiders.

This instinct is still strong and may be seen in the present-day dog, and means that many different breeds make excellent guard dogs. Up until several years ago, we had always had a dog in the family. Each animal was of a different breed, yet each showed this territorial instinct. Initially the dogs would behave aggressively to anyone approaching the house until cordially greeted by a member of the family. Then they would, sometimes reluctantly, accept the stranger as a new member of the 'pack' – the family.

Photographic reference

Dogs are very active animals, particularly the younger ones. I remember the last dog we had loved to play with a balloon. We would toss it into the air and he would jump up and try to grab it in his teeth. Another interesting action pose he got into was suddenly to roll on to his back for a few seconds and just as suddenly jump up again.

It would be almost impossible to capture such behaviour on paper, as it was happening. Apart from the sheer physical difficulty of having to draw quickly enough to produce any marks at all, there is also the impossibility of being in the right place at the right time with the right equipment! This is where a camera can be an invaluable tool. I have seen numerous photographs showing just this type of action.

> ## Artist's Tip
>
> *Whenever you use photographic reference, remember, as always, that you are dealing with a three-dimensional animal so construct it as such, building it up with guidelines and contour lines, as you would if you were drawing from life.*

This sleeping Labrador puppy *(above)* 'posed' for long enough to allow me to work in a precise medium, in this case pen and ink.

When drawing 'action' poses such as this rolling dog *(right)*, try to use a medium that will allow you to work loosely, producing free-flowing lines that convey a sense of movement. Work quickly, even when drawing from photographs – but only as quickly as you feel comfortable in doing. For this drawing I used a chisel pencil.

I used a 2B charcoal pencil on watercolour paper for this drawing. The pencil gave me a range of shades, from black to light grey. When used on a rough surface, it produced a bold effect which was ideal for conveying the aggressive display of this dog.

Odd angles

Even with the help of photographic reference, however, this type of behaviour can be difficult to portray convincingly because dogs are not normally seen from these angles and so, when they are, they have a tendency to look odd. If you practise drawing from different and unusual viewpoints, you will become more familiar with the whole shape of the dog and not merely the usual overhead views.

Showing expression

Dogs are intelligent and consequently very emotional animals, capable of showing a range of feeling from angry aggression to total submission. There are, however, certain breeds which seem perpetually to show one particular expression; this is not due to an emotional state, however, but merely to the facial characteristics of the dog.

To add to the confusion, you will find that certain features behave in the same way when a dog is displaying different emotions. You will only be able to guess the true emotion by looking at how the features combine. For example, a dog will lay back its ears when showing aggression, when frightened, and when being submissive. It will also reveal aggressiveness or fear by baring its top teeth, but it will either keep its mouth closed or open it just slightly when showing submission. So, to portray a particular emotion, you will have to understand and correctly combine several elements such as ears, eyes and posture.

A word of caution here: just because a dog is frightened does not mean that it is harmless. A frightened dog is a dangerous dog, so take care.

Eating and drinking

To start with, it would be sensible to choose something less challenging than a dog jumping or rolling about on the ground. A dog in the process of eating or drinking would make a good subject.

I realize that dogs have a tendency to devour their food in a matter of seconds, but this time can be greatly extended by giving the dog something to chew or gnaw at. This could be one of the artificial bones made of an extremely hard, edible, meat-flavoured substance available in some pet shops, but anything that the dog cannot gulp down and therefore would have to take time in consuming would serve the purpose. This would give you the chance to choose your viewpoint and either do one carefully measured drawing, putting in as much detail as possible, or to do two or three quick sketches from different angles.

A dog will invariably lie down when gnawing at a bone, but will stand when drinking or eating soft food, so you will have to bear this in mind when deciding which situation to set up.

Flexible medium

Because of its flexibility, watercolour is an excellent medium to use for portraying dogs involved in different types of behaviour. It is a medium which I enjoy using a great deal, for it has an aesthetic quality which I like very much. You can be exact with it, keeping it tight to produce realistic, detailed work, or use it loosely to produce fresh, free-flowing work. I also like to combine it with coloured pencils, drawing over the watercolour with pencil to sharpen up or emphasize details.

For this 'Jack Russell' terrier, I did a quick pencil drawing, keeping the lines light, paying particular attention to the shape of the eyes and nose, etc. I then finished the study with watercolour using a no. 6 Prolene brush on watercolour paper.

To draw this Chien, I used a felt-tip pen. It is a good tool to choose when you want to draw quickly, and can be used on both smooth and rough surfaces. I prefer one that has been in use for some time because it will have lost its new-ink quality and so will produce a more subtle line.

Working from life

If you decide to go out-of-doors in search of suitable subjects, limit yourself to one medium only to begin with. For example, if you choose to work in pencil, then take only one medium-grade pencil (say a B), a sharpener and, of course, a sketchbook. You will not need an eraser: if you feel you have made a mistake by drawing a line in the wrong place, simply draw it again in the right place. You can, if necessary, erase the incorrect one later, but I would leave it, for it will show you where you went wrong and how you corrected it – which is all part of the learning process.

You can add to your outdoor equipment as you gain experience and become more confident about working out in parks or whatever your chosen location. In the meantime, however, avoid cluttering yourself up with unnecessary gear until you have tried out the various media available, to find out which you prefer.

Artist's Tip

When doing a pastel drawing, like that of the Bassett Hound, you might overwork it by placing too many colours on top of each other. If so, spray with fixative and, when dry, work over your drawing again.

This Bassett Hound *(left)* is a perfect example of how the physical characteristics of some breeds give them a fixed expression – the Bassett's floppy ears, droopy eyes, and hanging jowls make it look permanently lugubrious. I produced this drawing on the matt side of brown wrapping paper, using just two pastels – a white and dark brown – with the paper representing the middle tone.

I found the fluid quality of water-soluble coloured pencil perfect for this quick sketch of a 'Jack Russell' tugging at its lead *(above)*.

Classic canine behaviour: two dogs sniff each other in greeting *(below)*. Capture such fleeting moments in sketch form first, then add to them later with, say, an ink wash, as here.

Movement

A running or jumping dog simply moves too quickly for the eye to follow, and is therefore impossible to draw from life. The parts that move most rapidly are the legs. Their position is constantly changing and, in fact, follows a strict sequence made up of a whole series of small, individual movements, rather like the frames in a cartoon film. All this happens too fast for the human eye to capture – but not too fast for the lens of a camera.

Single frames
Before the invention of photography, people simply had to guess at the way in which the legs and torso of different animals moved. Now, with the help of photographs, videos and television, people are able to 'freeze' these sequences of dogs and other animals in motion, and so identify exactly what is happening at any moment and – perhaps most importantly – how the separate movements all synchronize.

You may, through lack of experience, feel incompetent and therefore lack confidence in tackling dramatic movement at the outset. If so, practise on walking rather than running or jumping dogs. This drawing of a Lurcher is an example of what I mean. It is walking slowly toward something which obviously interests it. A situation like this could be set up, or a friend could be persuaded to walk a dog on a lead.

At first, just study the movement of the legs. Only when you feel that you understand the movement should you start to draw. This drawing was done in conté crayon on semi-rough cartridge paper.

I remember seeing a series of photographs taken with a camera normally used for sporting action shots – the type that automatically takes individual pictures in rapid succession. The result was a series of stills clearly showing the sequence of movements a dog goes through when it leaps up in the air to catch a ball from a standing position.

Drawing from memory
If you are drawing from life, the best method I have found is to spend some time simply observing your subject without drawing anything. Then, while the information is still fresh in your mind, quickly put down on paper everything that you can remember.

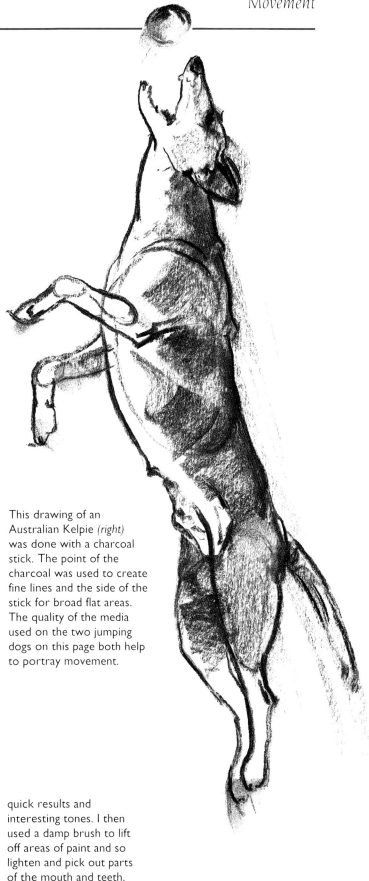

I drew this terrier *(above)* on a semi-rough cartridge paper using a no. 6 Prolene brush and black watercolour paint, a medium which produces quick results and interesting tones. I then used a damp brush to lift off areas of paint and so lighten and pick out parts of the mouth and teeth.

This drawing of an Australian Kelpie *(right)* was done with a charcoal stick. The point of the charcoal was used to create fine lines and the side of the stick for broad flat areas. The quality of the media used on the two jumping dogs on this page both help to portray movement.

179

The rhythms of movement

When you are drawing a moving dog, try not to think in terms of producing a perfect, finished drawing. What you are doing is primarily an exercise, the purpose of which is to capture the essence of the dog's body movement. You are looking for the rhythms in the body – the flowing sweep of lines and angles. If you can get these rhythms down first, concentrating just on the basic shapes, you can always add in details later, if required.

Large and loose

Paying too much attention to detail will distract you from the essentials of movement. To maintain more of an over-view and to get as much movement into your lines as possible, it's best to draw quickly – and large. This will give you the freedom of movement to produce the 'action' lines. Take care, however, to choose a scale with which you feel comfortable: if you force yourself to draw unnaturally large, this will only inhibit rather than liberate your style.

The first stage of this drawing of a running Foxhound (left) was a simple pencil sketch which was then completed by quickly blocking in, using white and very dark brown pastels. Treating the subject in this free, sketchy way adds greatly to the feeling of movement.

In this watercolour drawing of a swimming Springer Spaniel (above), a feeling of movement is not instantly apparent because the dog is viewed head-on and its legs – the greatest indicator of movement – are hidden. The fluid quality of the medium, however, the spreading, floating ears, and the disturbed water surface all contribute to a subtle sense of motion.

Artist's Tip

When you are trying to get movement into your lines, don't force the pace but draw as quickly as is comfortably possible. With practice, you will automatically begin to draw faster and with greater confidence.

The movement of this Border Collie as it leaps the fence *(left)* is almost identical, in three-quarter view, to the running movement of the dog below. It was drawn in felt-tip brush-pen.

A dog walking, trotting and running *(below)*. In the middle drawing, the dog's legs are bent more than in walking and its front foot is slightly off the ground, giving it a springy bounce. The running dog at the end is effectively doing a series of controlled leaps as it bounds along.

Focusing on the parts

Instead of trying to draw a whole dog to begin with, you could, if you prefer, first focus your attention on individual parts of the body. For example, you could study how the front leg bends and how the angle between top and bottom parts changes as the dog walks. How about the difference in angle between the head and neck? As your confidence grows, you could then tackle the whole body – remembering, as always, to build up your drawing from the basic shapes, lines and angles.

If you practise this system, eventually your observation, understanding and memory will improve sufficiently to enable you to reproduce – with a degree of accuracy – most of the different body shapes in movement.

A new angle

When you feel more confident in portraying movement, try a new challenge – drawing dogs from different angles. You could perhaps attempt drawing a dog from a low viewpoint, which involves looking up at the animal from underneath as it leaps into the air to retrieve a thrown object; or you could draw a dog running either towards you or away from you. Your earlier practice in drawing individual parts in motion can prove invaluable here.

This charcoal pencil drawing of a Poodle really epitomizes speed. The bold, almost scratchy quality of the lines creates a very dynamic sense of motion.

Artist's Tip

Drawing a dog from an unusual viewpoint can be tricky. However, if you develop a firm grasp of the rules of foreshortening, you will be able to produce a convincing drawing. These rules apply whether the animal is moving or still.

Sketching

Whatever art or craft you wish to pursue, the only way to improve your skills is by practice. For the artist, sketching is an excellent way of developing drawing skills and, as such, is an important part of the learning process: not only does it sharpen your powers of observation, but it also builds up your knowledge and understanding of structure and form.

Sketching styles
Sketching can take various forms. You may, for example, use your sketchbook to make quick scribbled drawings in an attempt to capture movement. Alternatively, you could do detailed drawings of various parts of the body to be used for future reference, thereby improving your knowledge of anatomy.

You could also use sketching as a way of experimenting with and learning more about different media and techniques.

I used a ballpoint pen for these two sketches. The smooth-running nature of ballpoint makes it a very suitable medium for producing quick drawings.

Artist's Tip

If you want to do some quick drawings on very rough paper, be sure to choose an instrument that will flow smoothly over the surface without getting snagged. For instance, it would be unwise to use a sharp, pointed nib on a very rough watercolour-type paper when you are trying to work at speed.

Brush-pen allowed for rapid sketching of this brief moment in time – sa Scottish Terrier begging for its ball *(below)*.

I used liquid acrylic paint to produce this sketch of a Welsh Springer *(above)*. I applied it with a no. 6 Prolene brush in my watercolour sketchpad. This versatile, sensitive medium can be used directly from the pot to produce strong, dark tones or watered down for a more subtle effect. Additionally you can use it to cover a large area quickly and to produce fine lines when required.

Artist's Tip

Never throw away or destroy your old sketchbooks. They could be of some help to you at a later date, and will also be a fascinating indicator of how your drawing is progressing.

Good practice

Try to get into the habit of carrying a sketchbook of convenient size and some basic drawing tools around with you whenever you can – this is good artist's practice. Then, should you unexpectedly spot something you would really like to jot down on paper, you will have everything you need at hand.

As well as being good drawing practice, the drawings you do in your sketchbook can also provide invaluable reference when you are unsure of what a particular feature looks like, and need more information.

Composition

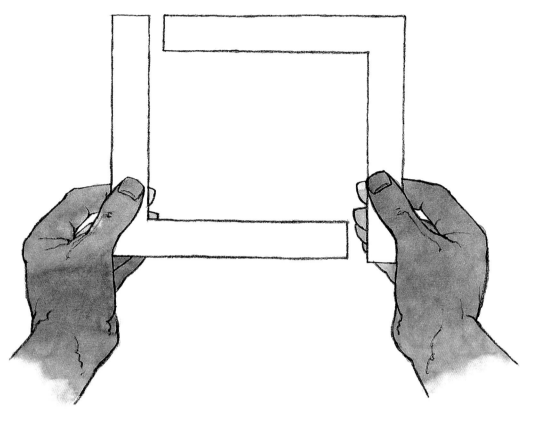

'Framing' your subject or composition is a useful technique when deciding on your arrangement. First cut out two corners from card, as long as you want, then turn them into a frame by holding them together at right angles. By sliding these two pieces together or pulling them apart, you will be able to establish the shape and proportion of the area taken up by your subject (left). This will help you when planning your drawing on your paper.

Laying down a larger version of the corners over your drawing will also help you decide on the size and proportions of your mount and/or frame (below).

The term 'composition' is used to describe the arrangement of various elements so that they produce a balanced picture which is pleasing to the eye. When composing your picture, it is helpful to bear a few general rules in mind.

Deciding what to include

One of the first rules is that you don't have to include everything you see. For example, you may, after studying a group of dogs, or people and dogs, decide to leave out one or more because doing so would improve the composition. You may even consider moving a dog or person to a different position.

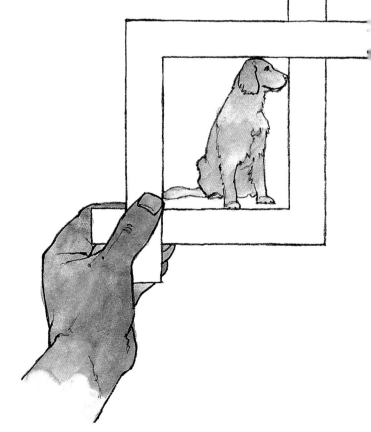

You would not be 'cheating' by doing this – on the contrary, you would be creatively making the arrangement more interesting or even exciting. The same principles apply when drawing a single dog. You could omit or underplay certain areas in order to concentrate on one particular part, such as the head.

The focal point

Every composition should have a particular area or spot to which the eye is drawn because of its special visual quality, or because the arrangement of the other elements in your picture leads to it. This is the 'focal point'.

Imagine, for example, that you are looking at a row of people at a dog show. Each has, on a lead, a small, dark-coloured dog with the exception of one, who has a large, light-coloured Great Dane. Your eye would be drawn to this dog because it is different from the others, making it the focal point of the group.

In this composition *(below)*, the woman with her dog on the far left is what first draws the eye, forming an off-centre focal point. The eye then travels the diagonal formed by the other groups to the sketchily drawn clump of trees, which balances the other elements without competing for attention.

If this dog were at the very end of the row, it would make for an uncomfortable arrangement, so it would be better to move it to a more central position. This focal point could be further accentuated by, say, making the clothes of the handler brighter than the rest.

Off-centre interest

By suggesting that you move the dog further into the picture, I don't necessarily mean *literally* into the centre – this would be too obvious. Your picture would look more interesting if the dog were positioned slightly to one side of centre.

A central focal point can be successful, but it needs to be handled with great care and thought to avoid it looking too contrived.

Artist's Tip

Never immediately accept the arrangement you see in front of you. Try looking at it from another position or, if you have a group formation, study it to see if there is a better composition contained within the group. Use the framing method to help you.

In Setting

When you are doing a study drawing of a dog, your intention is to learn more about the structure of the animal, its surface texture, etc, so its surroundings will not be important. You might also draw just the head if you want a drawing to frame and display on the wall. As a general rule, however, including some of the animal's surroundings will add to, rather than detract from, your drawing.

Finding your location
There are many places you can go to find dogs in different settings. For example, there are dog kennels scattered all over the country which you could look up in a local telephone directory. Other locations where you can find your subjects include dog obedience classes, which are sometimes advertised in the local press. Check first to find out whether your presence will be welcome; a polite phone call requesting permission for a short visit to carry out a little sketching or photography may prove successful.

This drawing of a Welsh Corgi at a dog show *(right)* was drawn with pastels on Ingres paper. This paper can be bought in the form of a flip-over pad, in various sizes, making it convenient to carry about. The area behind the Corgi was kept simple to avoid interference with the visual importance of the dog itself.

1 This drawing of a dog being trained as a guidedog for a blind person was done with a 4B pencil on semi-rough cartridge paper. I chose the length of the person's head (A) as my measuring unit to check the accuracy of the proportions before adding any detail. To check the angles of the arm, harness and the body of the dog, I held my pencil vertically (B). Including the fence and pavement had the effect of anchoring the dog and handler in their setting, thereby preventing them floating off into space.

2 When I was happy that the basic outlines, angles and perspective were correct, I was able to erase unwanted marks and add in the detail.

Other sources

Dog shows are another possible place to find your subject matter, and here there will be a huge variety of breeds to choose from. Another advantage of shows is that the dogs are required to stand still while on display, and so make good models. Dog races are another possibility, although here the only dogs will be greyhounds – often moving at impossibly high speeds!

If you are unable to get such direct access to your subject matter, you may have parkland or an area of waste ground near you where people frequently walk and exercise their dogs. You may also have friends or acquaintances who are dog owners. And if all else fails there are always the books in the local library, but do try to work from life if at all possible.

A quick pen-and-ink sketch was all that could be achieved when drawing this dog being held aloft (above). Notice, though, how it perfectly conveys the heaviness of the animal's posture and the downward droop of its head.

Loose brush-pen marks were whisked across the paper to depict this dog running after a boy with a ball (below). Observe how their shadows anchor them to the ground, and how just a single 'horizon line' behind them is enough to establish a setting.

This bitch peacefully feeding her puppies allowed the artist time to produce a fairly finished pencil drawing. A few sketchy lines convey the setting – the grassy spot on which the group sits.

Moving models

Greyhounds tearing along the racetrack move too fast for the naked eye to follow, but even with more placid subjects, movement is something you are going to have to contend with – the only time you can guarantee absolute stillness is when a dog is asleep. So don't be disappointed if your drawing isn't very finished. Try to establish the essentials in a good sketch. You can then build this up into a more complete drawing later. (Look, too, at the section on *Movement* on pages 178–83.)

Thinking about safety

When doing location work, always bear safety in mind. Listen to any advice given you as to where you should and should not go, for, apart from the possibility of an accident with the dogs themselves, there may be machinery or electrical apparatus in the vicinity which could be potentially dangerous.

Artist's Tip

It is good practice to take along some cover paper or tissue and adhesive tape when doing location work. Then, instead of having to use fixative, which can be ineffective in windy or even breezy conditions, you could cover your work with the paper, held in place on four sides with pieces of tape, to protect it until you can spray it.

Index